PRAISE FOR **THE GOOD FIGHT**

"In this terrific book, Liane Davey delivers a surprising and bracing message: Conflict is good for us. It can improve performance, help teams bond, and enrich the workplace. What matters is how you harness conflict to address tough topics and make hard decisions. If you feel like your organization is mired in a rut, you might need a good fight—and you definitely need *The Good Fight*."

DANIEL H. PINK, author of *When* and *Drive*

"Liane Davey has long been a secret weapon of the C-Suite. With *The Good Fight*, any leader can learn how to get their teams unstuck and working together again. Through humor and practical examples, Liane's book shows how even the most conflict-avoidant leaders can use productive conflict to resolve the issues that have been holding them back. Save yourself the stress and start applying her methods today."

SHAWN LAYDEN, chairman, Sony Interactive Entertainment Worldwide Studios

"For most leaders and teams, conflict is treated as something to avoid at all costs—instead of a path toward greater understanding, engagement, and success. Through practical examples, Davey gives us the right words so we might approach conflict as an ally rather than an adversary. I highly recommend *The Good Fight* for anyone leading a team. As many of us would agree, normalizing healthy conflict in the workplace is something that is long overdue."

DR. MARLA GOTTSCHALK, industrial/organizational psychologist and LinkedIn Influencer

"*The Good Fight* is an essential field guide that any leader can use to prevent drama before it starts. Davey provides practical and repeatable processes you can use to disarm people's egos, resolve the conflicts on your team, and restore sanity to your organization."

CY WAKEMAN, drama researcher, *New York Times*–bestselling author of *No Ego*, and founder of reality-based leadership

"Whether you're an organization of 10 or 10,000, the best solutions emerge when people feel comfortable sharing their ideas, even when what they have to say challenges the status quo. In *The Good Fight*, Davey shows leaders how to facilitate the productive, healthy conflict that's needed for teams to fully engage and give their best to the organization."

HOWARD BEHAR, former president, Starbucks International, and author of *It's Not about the Coffee: Lessons on Putting People First from a Life at Starbucks*

"We feel the pain of having a conflict immediately. But the pain of avoiding a conflict is insidious and invisible, like a toxic gas. In *The Good Fight*, Liane Davey shows us how to clear the air without causing an explosion."

KIM SCOTT, *New York Times*–bestselling author of *Radical Candor: Be a Kick-Ass Boss without Losing Your Humanity*

"Growing up among eight siblings, my mother always taught me to 'use my words, not my fists' whenever there was conflict. This advice not only helped me out of a jam, but taught me not to back down if things needed to be said. Productive conflict resolution had begun! In Liane Davey's new book, *The Good Fight*, she uses her twenty-five years of team-building experience to effectively teach people how to resolve conflict the right way—head on! Her practical strategies are purposeful and wise, and will help create healthy habits, build trust within your team, and increase the bottom line! An excellent read!"

DAVID M.R. COVEY, coauthor of *Trap Tales: Outsmarting the 7 Hidden Obstacles to Success*

THE GOOD FIGHT

THE GOOD FIGHT

Use Productive Conflict to Get Your Team and Organization Back on Track

LIANE DAVEY

PAGE TWO
BOOKS

Cataloguing in publication information is available from Library and Archives Canada.

ISBN 978-1-989025-20-8 (hardcover)
ISBN 978-1-989025-21-5 (ebook)

Page Two Books
www.pagetwo.com
Jacket and cover design by Peter Cocking
Interior design by Taysia Louie
Printed and bound in Canada by Friesens

Some names and identifying details have been changed to protect the privacy of individuals.

19 20 21 22 23   5 4 3 2 1

Distributed in Canada by Raincoast Books
Distributed in the US and internationally by Publishers Group West, a division of Ingram

LianeDavey.com

For Craig, Kira, and Mac—
who are worth fighting for

≋ CONTENTS ≋

≡ INTRODUCTION ≡

HI. **IT'S NICE** to meet you.

In this book, we're going to dive into relationships and communication, so I thought it would help if we get to know each other.

I'll go first. I'm Liane. I advise teams on how to be more effective.

Studying teams, and more specifically what makes teams effective, has been a professional passion for more than twenty-five years. My fascination with how teams work (and how they fail) dates back to grade school. My sixth grade teacher, Mrs. Fahey, assigned us to create our own Caribbean country. It was a great project with assignments covering geography, social sciences, language, and math. It even had artistic components: we were asked to write a national anthem and create a flag. It was right up my alley. I still love that kind of multifaceted project.

The only problem was that the project would be done in groups. We were assigned to work with two classmates and told we would each receive the same mark. It didn't take long for me to realize this arrangement was going to cramp my style. From the first work session, my teammates made it clear that they were happy to cruise through with minimal effort. My idea to use papier-mâché to build a 3-D topographical map seemed a little too ambitious for them. At twelve years old, I was already learning how hard it is to work on a team.

I figured I had two choices. I could do the majority of the work, which would ensure the project was up to my standards. That would give me the mark I was looking for but would create a huge workload for me. Even at that age, the unequal allocation offended my sensibilities. How was it fair if I did all the work and my teammates received the same grade? The other option was to dole out the work equally and let my mark take a hit. That option felt more equitable in terms of workload, but it didn't seem fair that I would have to settle for a lower mark. I decided to do the work to get the good grade.

When I tell people this story, many of them regale me with their own versions. Whether they first experienced the struggle of teamwork in grade school, at Scouts, or at sleepaway camp, or whether it took until their first MBA class or day one in the workplace, everyone has a story of that moment when they realized teamwork can really suck. Faced with their first crappy team, most people make the same binary decision I did: either do all the work to get the desired result or live with the consequences of sharing the work equally.

In 1993, I decided to turn my personal interest in teamwork into my professional path to see if I could find a third option. I earned a PhD in organizational psychology—the study of behavior in the workplace. My dissertation research focused on how team dynamics affect innovation, and pretty much everything I've done since then has centered on more effective teamwork. All these years after sixth grade, I'm confident that I've found the third option: conflict. We can fight to make our teams better: better ideas, better decisions, better execution, better results.

The trouble is that fighting to make our teams better is still fighting. And in twenty-five years of studying and advising teams, I've learned over and over again that we don't like to fight.

That's where I come in. I've dedicated my career to helping people get over their conflict aversion and start fighting the good fight.

Okay, that's me. Now it's your turn.

Let me guess. You're a strong performer who has always done well at work. You've already had multiple promotions based on your ability to get things done efficiently. You're used to being self-reliant and you're not afraid of a little hard work. But lately, you're finding it more difficult to get things done. So many of your assignments require you to work with folks who just don't seem to get it—or maybe they have their own priorities that don't mesh well with yours. This problem is especially challenging when you have to work on cross-functional teams where everyone is serving a different master. It sure makes it hard to collaborate effectively.

You think about this problem of collaboration a lot, but you haven't figured out how to talk about it with your teammates without getting everyone upset. And that's the last thing you want! It's hard enough to get things done without all the office drama that seems to erupt when you suggest that maybe the team could do things a little differently. But saying nothing isn't working either, so you're thinking maybe it's time to take the risk.

You believe there must be a way to work through all the competing priorities to get your team focused on the right stuff—the short list of actions that will make the biggest difference. There must be a way to deal with the aggressive people, the passive people, and maybe even the passive-aggressive people who are all eroding trust on your team. There must be a way to reduce the toll that poor teamwork is taking and actually get back to business.

There is a way.

The answer to all of those problems is to embrace productive conflict and start fighting the good fight. This book will walk you through the steps.

In Part I, we'll focus on the business case for conflict. We'll start by talking about all the ways that avoiding the tough discussions and decisions holds your business back, makes your team dysfunctional, and causes you stress. We'll look at the notion of "conflict debt," the gap that's created when you try to avoid the contentious issues that need to be resolved. Then we'll identify all the reasons why you're avoiding those conflicts in the first place. Finally, we'll try on a new mindset about conflict—one that sees conflict as healthy for your bottom line, your relationships, and your stress level.

In Part II, we'll focus on the mechanics of productive conflict. You'll learn how you can proactively establish a line of communication and build trust with your colleagues. Next, you'll learn techniques to create a strong connection that turns adversaries into allies. Finally, you'll gain practical strategies for how to short-circuit unproductive or adversarial conflict and start to contribute to a solution. You'll realize that it's possible to prevent the majority of conflicts and make those you can't prevent more productive and less aversive.

In Part III, we'll look at ways to help your team systematize conflict, so it becomes a natural part of how you work. We'll start with a process for clarifying expectations that neutralizes the majority of conflicts by increasing alignment and reducing miscommunication. Next, we'll look at how you can normalize the tensions often present in teams, so your discussions stay focused on business issues rather than becoming personal. Finally, we'll discuss a variety of techniques to build a healthy conflict habit on your team.

In the Bonus Chapter, we'll apply your new productive conflict skills to your most important relationships: the ones at home. We'll talk about the role of productive conflict in a healthy partnership and your responsibility to model these skills to the children in your life. We'll move outside the home, too, applying productive conflict to volunteer teams and the community.

Throughout the book, I'll share stories of my clients (disguised to protect their identities) and how they learned to use productive conflict to make their businesses more profitable and more innovative, their teams more trusting and more fun, and their own lives more rewarding and less stressful. It wouldn't be fair if I left myself out of this story—to show you that I've gone through exactly the same journey, I'll share my stories of learning and applying productive conflict skills.

I'm so glad you're here.

PART I

THE CASE FOR CONFLICT

1

CONFLICT DEBT

A **GROUP OF DOCTORS** sits around a mahogany table in a luxurious private club. It's a sunny Saturday morning at 8 o'clock and while most people are at the club for the tennis or the eggs Benedict, we're crammed into a meeting room discussing the lackluster growth of these doctors' medical practice. I've been hired to help them work through their issues and get the business back on a growth trajectory.

They aren't talking much. They're barely making eye contact. They know they need to be here and have willingly sacrificed a day off to have these conversations, but it's clear they would rather be anywhere else. How could working through a few business decisions be so hard? It's not brain surgery! In fact, brain surgery would be way easier for some of them than leading their fifty-person organization.

It gets worse before it gets better. Just ahead of the morning break, we broach a topic that's so raw that the group has been avoiding it for months. In my head, I'm singing the kids' song "We're Going on a Bear Hunt." You know the one: "We can't go over it, we can't go under it, we gotta go through it!" So I wade in. Apparently not everyone is ready to go through it. One doctor is so upset by the conversation that she closes her notebook, gives us a piece of her mind, and then storms out. One of the partners who organized the day races after her, but he can't convince her to return.

At the break, two of the female partners corner me in the ladies' room to convince me to raise another sensitive issue that's been left undiscussed. This one is about the unfairness of how they distribute shifts. They give me ten years of history through the stall door. The male partners, lacking the ladies' room ambush option, resort to sending lengthy emails about these and other festering topics.

After only a few hours, it's clear to me what's wrong. As we return from lunch, I share my diagnosis: "You need more conflict."

What?! They look at each other, confused. *Did she just say* more *conflict?* On the plus side, at least I have them making eye contact now. More conflict is the *last* thing they expect me to say. They are already in agony dealing with the smallest decisions. Each meeting is an excruciating cocktail of trepidation, anger, guilt, and frustration. How could they possibly need *more* conflict?

What they don't realize is that they're mired in all those negative emotions because they're unwilling to work *through* them. As long as they avoid the topics that are creating the anger, guilt, and frustration, they are stuck with them. They are ignoring Winston Churchill's adage, "If you're going through hell, keep going." Several topics on the table have been there not just for weeks or months but for years. They have tried every which way to go *around* the contentious issues, but now they need to go *through* them.

The Importance of Conflict

The doctors are not the only ones who avoid conflict. Most of us have been raised to think of conflict as a bad thing—something to be avoided when building a healthy organizational culture. Conventional wisdom holds that conflict is bad for productivity and corrosive to trust and engagement. Unfortunately, that view is totally at odds with how an organization actually works. Conflict isn't bad for organizations: it's fundamental to them. The ability to work through

WHILE ORGANIZATIONS REQUIRE

• CONFLICT, •

HUMANS TEND TO

➤ RUN FROM IT. ◄

THE RESULT IS

⹀ CONFLICT DEBT. ⹀

opposing sides of an issue and come to a resolution in the best interest of customers, shareholders, and employees is required on a daily basis by everyone—from the boardroom to the shop floor. Conflict is part of strategic planning, resource allocation, product design, talent management, and just about everything else that happens in an organization. Or at least everything that *should* happen in an organization.

Unfortunately, it doesn't always happen as it should. While organizations require conflict, humans tend to run from it. Rather than working through the conflicts that will help our organizations move forward, we avoid, postpone, evade, duck, dodge, and defer them. The result is conflict debt.

Conflict Debt

Conflict debt is the sum of all the contentious issues that need to be addressed to be able to move forward but instead remain undiscussed and unresolved. Conflict debt can be as simple as withholding the feedback that would allow your colleague to do a better job and as profound as continually deferring a strategic decision while getting further and further behind the competition.

The doctors are in conflict debt. Each time they avoid the discussions, debates, and disagreements that are needed to get their business growing again, they sink further in. I mention the notion of conflict debt and one of the doctors smiles wryly and admits, "I call it the 'too hard' pile." *Yes*, I think, *he's nailed it!* He proceeds to itemize a list of contentious issues that they have been tacitly agreeing to ignore and attempting to work around. Their "too hard" pile is so high and contains so many issues to be avoided that every avenue of growth has been obstructed by something undiscussable.

To understand where conflict debt comes from, think of financial debt. You get into financial debt when you use credit to buy things you otherwise can't afford. You want something, maybe even need it, but it's too expensive or you don't have the cash at the time, so you use credit. You rationalize to yourself that you will pay it off as soon as you get your next paycheck, but if you're like 65% of American credit card holders,[1] you carry that balance over from month to month. The debt mounts, and over time, it gets harder and harder to get out from under it.

As with financial debt, conflict debt starts off innocently. An issue comes up that's a little too hot to handle, so you defer it. You promise yourself that you'll revisit it when things are less busy, or when cooler heads prevail (i.e., when pigs fly or hell freezes over). You buy yourself time and space. But days pass, and no spontaneous resolution materializes. Instead, the issue becomes more contentious and the factions more entrenched. Suddenly, you're in conflict debt. You're feeling anxious, trying to avoid the topic, and maybe even steering clear of your colleagues to avoid having to confront the issue. (Have you ever taken the long way around the office so you don't run into a disgruntled colleague?) Although you're glad to be avoiding the conflict, you're feeling frustrated at the lack of progress, not to mention a little guilty for your role in the stalemate. Conflict debt weighs you down.

Avoiding the *issue* is only one path to conflict debt. Another is to avoid the *opposition*. In this case, you broach the topic but exclude people who might disagree or cause tension, surrounding yourself with those who are already onside. You focus on how congenial and productive the discussion is, deluding yourself that your solutions are going to fly with the people who were strategically disinvited. Pretending the opposition doesn't exist won't make it disappear. It will resurface when your opponents kill your plan or, worse, just leave it to fail. Ugh.

There's a third way to get into conflict debt: avoid the *friction*. Even if you discuss the difficult subject, there's still room to get yourself into trouble if you veer safely away from the distressing parts of the discussion. When you make it clear (either intentionally or inadvertently) that nothing antagonistic should taint your conversation, you start to rack up conflict debt. I see this all the time when, just as the discussion gets perilously close to the crux of the matter, someone suggests they "take it offline" to avoid having to deal with the conflict. Everyone smiles and pretends that they'll actually come back to it at some point and then returns to business as usual. Stifling dissent creates conflict debt.

I know each of these techniques personally. I have a long track record as a conflict avoider. I concocted all sorts of stories to make myself feel better about my choice to avoid conflict. I deferred important discussions and reassured myself that it would be easier to broach the uncomfortable topic later. I excluded the people who would challenge me and rationalized that I was just gaining momentum for my plan. I stifled the really unpleasant conversations but still checked the box pretending my idea had actually been vetted. Are you avoiding the conflicts that your organization requires you to work through? If so, you are setting your organization, your team, and yourself up for trouble.

Identify the Conflict Debt in Your Business

Conflict debt can cripple organizations in different ways. How does it show up in your organization? Here are a few examples of the forms it can take.

Poor Prioritization

If I had to guess which of the common forms of conflict debt harms your team the most, I'd go with failure to prioritize; it's the most prevalent of all conflict debts.[2] Your organization is likely trying to do more than time or resources permit, but no one is making a call about where to proceed, where to postpone, and where to pull the plug. Of course not! Making that decision would require leaders to pit one project, one department, or one person against another—a potentially messy conflict. Instead of hashing out what matters most, leaders cascade long lists of priorities down through the organization. The need to prioritize doesn't disappear, it's simply delegated. Eventually, someone will have to decide about what to do first—maybe you.

The executive team of a large retail chain learned this lesson the hard way. The leaders are driven, and their ambition causes them to devalue prioritization. They continually con themselves into believing that they can (and must!) do everything all at once. When the executives from real estate, financial services, and corporate social responsibility each wanted to launch simultaneous initiatives that would require cashiers to impose on customers at the checkout, it was the executives' responsibility to work through the options and make a decision about which was most important. Instead, they let all three initiatives proceed, loath to battle over which project was more valuable than another.

The conflict among priorities didn't go away, it simply trickled down. The head of operations had an opportunity to resolve it, but she lacked the authority to unilaterally cancel another department's program or the appetite to engage the others in what she knew would be an adversarial discussion. So the conflict between departments that should have been resolved at the top of the organization moved deeper and deeper into the ranks until it reached the cashier.

Once the customer was at the cash register, the prioritization could no longer be postponed. It was now up to the cashier to prioritize. Imagine what it's like to be this cashier. The real estate team wants you to ask for customers' zip codes to plan the locations of new stores. Financial services is pushing a store credit card and expects you to solicit applications. The corporate social responsibility team wants you to request a donation to a children's charity.

You look up at the line of four customers with heaping carts waiting impatiently to check out: shoppers shifting uncomfortably, kids whining, parents checking their watches. You picture the tally board in the back of the store that shows how many zip codes, how many credit card applications, and how many donations came in on your shift. You know if you try to get all three, customer ratings of the shopping experience will tank, and you think to yourself, *Oh that will* definitely *hit the manager's bulletin board!* You attempt to prioritize the requests based on potential outcome: you do your best to size up each customer and guess which request will work best. Does a charitable donation trump a zip code? Is it best to make one request, or two, or three? Is getting all the information worth risking an angry customer? But this was never your decision to make.

The executives created a conflict debt that had to be paid off by junior employees. Decisions were made, just by someone with less context to make them well. When leaders fail to prioritize, they pass their conflict debt down the line. In this case, the executives created the debt and the cashiers and customers paid for it.

Employees and customers pay for conflict-avoidant executives all the time, but they aren't the only ones. Research shows that shareholders pay as well. In a longitudinal study[3] conducted by executive search firm ghSmart, the number one predictor of long-term CEO success was their willingness to make decisions earlier, faster, and with greater conviction, even amid ambiguity. In the study, people described as "decisive" were twelve times more likely to lead financially high-performing companies. Interestingly, of CEOs ousted from their companies for bad decision-making, there were twice as many fired for making *no* decisions than for making *bad* decisions. I do take some comfort in knowing that indecisive chief executives who create conflict debt by failing to prioritize eventually pay the price.

Innovation Silos

Failure to prioritize isn't the only form of conflict debt that suffocates your organization. Cultures that reject conflict forego the sometimes fiery interdepartmental mash-ups that are needed to generate new ideas. You shouldn't fear the fiery! It's normal that people from different departments will propose diverse approaches or advocate for different stakeholders, and it's natural that they will be passionate, frustrated, or angry if they don't feel those perspectives are valued. Leaders often avoid crossing silos to avoid this friction. Unfortunately, it's that friction that sparks innovation.

In some cases, avoiding these uncomfortable discussions only postpones the fight. One engineering team I worked with slaved away building a whizbang gizmo. They knew they could work faster and with less interference if they kept marketing and sales out of the loop, so they didn't tell anyone what they were working on. They didn't want early feedback that would affect their flow or productivity. They convinced themselves that they were just trying to use other departments' time wisely, but really they were trying to avoid conflict. Their approach did help them go faster, but it also sheltered them from the truth that their concept was flawed. It was not a happy day when the engineers eventually learned from marketing and sales that they would not be allocating people or budget to the sale of the product. I'm convinced that if sales, marketing, and the engineers had locked themselves in a room to hash it out from the beginning, the whizbang idea could have turned into a useful product.

When you work in a conflict-averse culture, everyone avoids the contentious conversations that create the conditions for successful innovation. The result is that nothing new or different ever emerges. Sure, incremental improvements come from within the silos, but the opportunity to harness differing perspectives to create something truly groundbreaking never materializes. Does your company have comfy, safe silos protecting you from conflict while starving you of innovation?

Hidden Risk

A less obvious but potentially costlier impact of organizational conflict aversion is that without conflict, it's almost impossible to identify and mitigate risks. In some cases, leaders refuse to seek contrary opinions because of pride of authorship: "How could there be anything wrong with our plan?" More commonly, it's not hubris, it's practicality. The team is up against the wall, barreling toward a looming deadline, naively (or not so naively) hoping everything will work out. There's no time to let a dissenting voice slow things down.

Plans need to be exposed to the people who can see them with fresh eyes, but that's the last thing most people want once they've invested so much time and energy in a project. It's easy to start believing the hype. Business school case studies are full of stories of teams that conveniently ignored warning signs on their path to failure. Avoiding the people and discussions that could expose flaws in a plan is a form of conflict debt.

This dynamic of hiding a plan from potential critics plays out frequently in organizations with risk and compliance functions—the groups charged with making sure the organization is following all laws and regulations and keeping the organization safe. I was working with an international wealth management team of a large bank. They were responsible for diversifying the global portfolio by driving 200% growth in assets under management outside of North America. They had to make difficult decisions about which countries to target and which to avoid. Some countries had attractive growth potential but volatile economic or political situations. The risk management team, who had experts on these issues, should have been involved. Instead, the wealth leaders were reluctant to involve folks from risk management in their discussions, referring to the head of risk as the "VP of business prevention" because it often felt like the only solution that would be safe enough for him was to sell nothing at all. By avoiding this conflict with the risk team about where it was safe to grow their business, the wealth team was essentially saying that they'd rather have their butts kicked by the market than by someone in their own organization.

Conflict debt, no matter what form, costs your organization dearly. Avoiding the stress-testing of the vetting process leaves you vulnerable to all manner of risks. Staying in siloes starves your organization of the diversity of thought that generates innovation. Failing to prioritize spreads your resources too thinly to have an impact.

The Interest

The direct costs of conflict debt are significant, but the indirect costs might be even higher. When you accumulate debt, you pay interest. You pay for the privilege of postponing payment. The same is true with conflict debt: the longer you leave the original problem unresolved, the more interest you pay. For example, if your organization fails to innovate, you pay when you have no way to compete, and you pay more as your most talented workers start to disengage. In fact, studies have shown that 68% of employees aren't as engaged as they could be.[4] If you refuse to prioritize, you pay when you fail to execute and pay again when you overburden and demoralize your workforce. When you shut out skepticism, you pay when you run into disaster and pay again as the cynicism grows in response to every crisis that could have and should have been foreseen and avoided. You pay for conflict debt over and over.

Such was the case with the doctors from the story at the start of the chapter. Some of the deferred decisions that had put them in conflict debt had been lingering for years. Some new members of the team weren't even part of the organization when the issues started. They had never heard of some of them, let alone had the opportunity to weigh in. The sad fact was that regardless of whether or not they were responsible for the conflict debt, they were paying for it in stalled growth and animosity, lack of trust, and a culture that now strongly resisted any attempts to get to the root of the problem.

Conflict Debt in Your Teams

Not all conflict debt stems from leaders sidestepping difficult business decisions. Teams can have conflict debt, too. You might be racking up debt on your team by avoiding uncomfortable interpersonal issues or putting up with dysfunctional team dynamics. If you let too many of these issues pile up, you'll find that most of the energy of your team is expended on the drama of team dysfunction, rather than on getting the job done. Are you ignoring any one of these issues that might be causing conflict to build up in your team?

Insufficient Skills

One prevalent form of team conflict debt is the failure to deal with perennially poor performers. I see many managers who knowingly allow the wrong people to sit around the table. Unfortunately, the whole team pays the price. Do you have someone on your team who doesn't belong there anymore? They might have been capable at some point, but now either their role has become negated by a new business model, their skills antiquated by advances in technology, or their energy simply worn down by the daily grind. You tell yourself you have no choice: "It will take six months to replace these skills. Better to have someone than no one," or "They've been here too long, it will cost too much to let them go," or "It's the CEO's son-in-law, I can't fire him!" If you are trying to avoid conflict with a poor performer, there are lots of excuses you can use to justify inaction. Just know that avoiding conflict with the poor performer is setting up conflict with everyone else.

For the members of your team who *are* performing, it can be irritating if you force them to drag along a teammate who is doing subpar work. You might be letting the whole team's reputation suffer because of one weak link.

Failing to deal with a poorly performing employee is demotivating to your good people. They are expected to pick up the slack with increased workloads, to work overtime when their teammate misses deadlines, or to invest an inordinate amount of time assisting their teammate with tasks that they should be able to do on their own ("Okay, Phyllis, one more time. This is how you transfer a phone call.") When you as a manager are unwilling to address poor performers, you create conflict for your strong performers. It's so backward, yet so common.

Bad Behavior

It's not only bad performance that can create conflict on a team. Bad behavior is a significant problem, too. One team I worked with exemplified the kind of vicious cycle that is created when a team leader puts up with bad behavior. This team was in a cost-competitive technology business and they were feeling the pressure from all sides. Frank, the head of sales, was doing his best to protect their prices, and Adam, the head of operations, was trying to find ways to trim the fat to protect their margins. Each department was fighting hard, but they had no line of sight to what their peers were doing to contribute to a solution. That made it easy for everyone to believe they were the only ones doing all the hard work while everyone else was slacking off.

One day, in front of the entire team, Frank unleashed his frustrations on Adam. Frank accused Adam of not being relentless enough on driving cost out of the product. His criticisms were dripping with condescension, suggesting Adam was too out of touch to understand just how behind he was. Not surprisingly, Adam became defensive and started to justify his choices, doling out lines like, "Someone here needs to think about quality!"

The rest of the team, including the team leader, saw the kernel of truth in Frank's tirade, but instead of getting the discussion back on track, they rushed to Adam's aid to take the sting out of Frank's personal attack. The nasty interpersonal dynamic diverted attention away from the underlying business issue—the shrinking margins. The team ended the day with no plan of action on the cost pressures, plenty of hard feelings about Frank, and a few lingering doubts about Adam.

The whole crisis was triggered because no one had been given the chance to stress-test Adam's plans, and Frank had no opportunity to air his concerns proactively. Conflict debt about the business compounded into conflict debt for the team. Ouch.

I often see managers allowing people to get away with atrocious behavior like Frank's that is toxic to everyone around them. This is particularly common if the offender is someone who gets good results. Bad behavior takes many forms: the shameless gossip, the sarcastic naysayer, or the self-aggrandizing loudmouth. Perhaps the most feared character is the aggressive dominant type who is quick to shout and blame. Having one of these on your team can create a dynamic anywhere on the continuum from an all-out, drop-the-gloves melee to a silenced majority where everyone lets the bully have his way. The most common reaction is somewhere in the middle: passive-aggressiveness.

If you've had to deal with the passive-aggressive spiral on your team, you know you have two troublemakers to deal with: the person whose aggressive behavior triggered the problem in the first place and the person who responded with guerilla warfare. It's tempting to conclude that they deserve each other and to leave well enough alone, but leaving this situation unchecked is a bad idea. In the absence of a proper forum to resolve the issue, the passive-aggressive person will continue to seethe. Everyone else will keep moving based on the overt signs that the situation is alright, only to be sideswiped by covert dissent somewhere down the road. If you're ignoring passive-aggressiveness on your team, expect progress to stall, trust to erode, and confidence to wane. Unfortunately, passive-aggressiveness is a particularly insidious problem for managers because the bad behavior can be hidden from you. You face a larger and larger bill for a debt you didn't know you had.

Nasty aggressive types obviously need to be dealt with. Vindictive passive-aggressive types clearly need to be addressed. But what about the people who play the victim? When you have bad behavior on your team, you're sure to also have wounded people. You'll know them by their woe-is-me attitude and their inability or unwillingness to stand up for themselves. Are you creating a conflict debt by letting the wounded people wallow around the office?

Failing to address the person who feels wronged by the goings-on in the team creates just as debilitating a debt as failing to deal with the more obvious anti-social behavior. The wounded person's colleagues have to endure considerable complaining and invest energy in trying to boost their demoralized coworker. If those attempts fail to placate them, it's common for the wounded person's frustration to boil over and for them to go on the attack. Now, unexpectedly, team members have to protect themselves from the person they were just trying to console. Enabling a victim mentality can cause problems for everyone.

You can see how conflict debt on your team can compound as one dysfunctional dynamic creates another. The aggressive person triggers the passive-aggressive one and vice versa. Either an aggressive or a passive-aggressive team member can evoke victim behavior in others. Now all of your energy is going into dealing with the drama instead of getting work done. It might even be too late to save your team in its current form. Once the interpersonal issues erode trust, it can be almost impossible to get it back.

Someone might need to leave the team for you to resurrect it. You might be surprised to learn that, in my experience, it's more likely to be the wounded person who needs to leave, not the aggressive one. Whereas the aggressive (or gossiping, or sarcastic) types can learn to use more constructive outlets for their concerns, those who feel wronged often lack the energy and resilience to make another earnest attempt at making the team better. They are exhausted by the experience and often past the point of no return.

Research suggests that interpersonal conflict debt on teams costs the economy billions of dollars as unresolved conflicts drive absenteeism rates up.[5] Stress due to interpersonal conflict also leads to short-term disability, which is both costly and disruptive to an organization. Another interesting side effect of the unwillingness or inability of managers to address the conflict debt is the greater reliance on external dispute mechanisms. Employees who see no internal path to problem resolution turn to external mediators, arbitrators, and even the courts, at significant time investment for managers and cost for the organization. Again, conflict debt gets paid one way or another.

The Cost to You Personally

We've talked about the negative effects of conflict debt on both your organization and your team. But conflict debt at the personal level takes an even greater toll. You get into conflict debt when you stifle your concerns, downplay your doubts, or fail to advocate on your own behalf. The interest paid on personal conflict debt can be debilitating: sleepless nights, self-doubt, and chronic stress.

I relate to this one personally. I quit my first job because I had a poisonous relationship with my boss and I was too conflict averse to deal with it. She was a strong, dominant woman with little empathy and less insight. I was terribly stressed out by our adversarial relationship. Not only was I attempting to navigate the politics for my own career, but I was a new manager and desperately trying to protect the people who reported to me. Being the shock absorber between her and my team left me depleted at the end of each day. By the time I got home, my husband and young daughter got little of my energy. I tossed and turned at night. In the end, I decided it was easier to leave than to work through my conflict debt—the equivalent of declaring bankruptcy.

I interviewed at multiple places to find a job where that kind of thing would never happen again. I found a great organization and a great boss. The first couple of years were fantastic. But slowly, my second team became dysfunctional, too. Now I wasn't just a manager, I was a leader, part of the team that was implementing big changes. We were merging groups, replacing leaders, revising strategy, moving offices—doing all the things that stress people out and bring out the worst in them. We saw passive behavior, aggressive behavior, passive-aggressive behavior—you name it, it was happening on our team.

I was in on the action as much as anyone. I was aggressively pushing for the new world order, not making room for members of my team to talk about legitimate resistance. I avoided the uncomfortable conversations and didn't do enough to make personal connections in response to the gossip going on behind closed doors. It was challenging, painful, and character building all over again. I was back to flopping down lifeless on the couch at night, neglecting my family (by this point I had two kids), and wondering how I was going to survive another thirty years of working. With all intent to do the opposite, I had racked up an unmanageable conflict debt, again!

Do you relate? Do you trudge through your work week, building up resentment about how you're being treated and engendering an equal amount of animus in others? It looks different for everyone, but the most common sources of individual conflict debt I see are: 1) taking on an overwhelming or unfairly distributed workload; 2) receiving insufficient or uneven opportunities for growth and development; and 3) tolerating inappropriate treatment from bosses and teammates. If you look in the mirror and tell yourself to "suck it up, buttercup," in response to one of the following issues, you're in conflict debt.

Workload

Have you taken on a greater and greater workload without pushing back? It happened to most of us during the great recession of 2008.

Organizations started stripping out people and divvying up their workload among those who remained. First, it was about survival, but over time, it became an obsession with higher growth at lower cost. Are you trudging along under the weight of an unreasonable workload? Are you underwater much of the time, constantly worried that you've dropped a ball? Each time your boss slinks toward your desk to drop off a new piece of work, do you smile grudgingly and add it to the pile? You really need to say "no" to this additional work, or at least get the boss to take something else off your plate, but at the moment, it seems easier to just add the unmanageable workload to your conflict debt. Surely, you'll be able to deal with it later.

One of my friends got a wakeup call about his workload from his young son. After several weeks of working nights and weekends, he hadn't had much quality time with his boys. One night, he managed to get home at a decent hour but continued to work on a proposal that was due the next day. His elder son approached him and asked, "If you can bring your computer, will you take me to the park?" That was enough to convince him that he needed to have a conversation with his boss about getting some additional help.

Development

Another conversation you might be putting off is the discussion about your opportunities for growth and development. Your manager never raises the issue, so you soldier on, doing the work but feeling as if you're ready for the next challenge. Business as usual suits your boss because you're good at your job and making life easy for her. But the longer you do a job you feel you've outgrown, the more frustrated you become. You're more disengaged each day. That's the price you pay when you don't advocate for yourself.

The longer you stay at the same level, without change, growth, or progress, the greater the debt. You pay in boredom, which makes the days feel endless. You pay in self-doubt as you wonder whether you'll ever get ahead. You pay in envy when you watch the people who play the political game better than you sail past. The longer you carry this debt, the more you start to believe that you don't have what it takes.

The voice in your head tells you your boss isn't offering you the cool opportunities because you're not worthy of them. When you get in a negative headspace, you're more likely to think that you're not worthy rather than realizing that you just never asked.

Treatment

Your conflict debt doesn't have to be about something as objective as your workload or your development. The costliest conflict debt can come from tolerating treatment that demoralizes you. How people interact with you has a huge impact on your experience of work, but it can be difficult to find a way to ask for what you need.

It happens in the simplest ways. I remember an office redesign at my former workplace. We were moving to an open environment, with rows of desks and no dividers. The introvert on the team, the one whose work required long stretches of quiet concentration, was now seated on the edge of the main thoroughfare through the office. Being a kind person, she would look up and smile as people walked by. The majority of people would meet her gaze and stop for a quick chat. While pleasant, this new arrangement was having a serious impact on her productivity. The longer it went on, the more frustrated she became with the constant interruptions. Taking one for the team wasn't helping anyone.

Putting the introvert in the high-traffic spot was an innocent oversight that was eventually rectified. Some clashes with your personal style are less innocuous. You might be the type of person who needs time to let ideas soak in before you're ready to add your full value. Faced with a manager who likes to spring things on you, expecting you to improvise an answer on the fly, you might splutter and stumble. You kick yourself when the most brilliant epiphany hits you an hour later. If you don't communicate your need for thinking time to your boss, you suffer with feeling inadequate every time he ambushes you, looking for your input.

You might cut yourself some slack when you struggle to confront your boss about how you're being treated, but you get more frustrated with yourself for letting your peers treat you poorly. Whether it's the person who always interrupts you in meetings, the one in the cubicle beside you who uses her "outside voice" on phone calls, or the one you caught whispering about you in the break room, walking away without saying anything leaves you in conflict debt with your coworkers. Now you're dealing with the impact of the original issue (getting cut off, distracted, or demeaned by your teammate's behavior) *and* your own frustration with yourself for putting up with such poor treatment.

Time to Make a Payment

Conflict debt is affecting your performance. At the organizational level, the unwillingness to work through uncomfortable situations is stretching resources too thinly, stifling innovation, and allowing risks to go unnoticed. On your team, the aversion to prickly conversations is forcing strong performers to compensate for weak ones and mature people to put up with immature ones. For you personally, the discomfort in advocating for yourself is leaving you burned out.

When your conflict debt gets too high, it becomes overwhelming. You're exhausted by the thought of trying to pay it off. You've destroyed your credit rating with your boss and your coworkers by letting these issues go unresolved for so long. Maybe it's so bad that you're tempted to declare bankruptcy and move to a new team to get a fresh start like I did. Don't give up—there are many things you can do to get out from under your conflict debt.

In Brief

- Organizations require conflict to operate. From developing a strategic plan to doling out constructive feedback, being part of an organization means you will need to work through uncomfortable situations.

- Conflict debt builds up when you avoid the discussions and decisions that are required. It can result when you sidestep contentious issues, shut out opposing voices, or keep conversations safely above the real problems.

- With conflict debt, the principal costs are compounded by the interest that accumulates in the form of frustration, disengagement, and eroded trust.

- Conflict debt is costly to organizations. The unwillingness to work through organizational conflicts prevents effective prioritization, creates innovation silos, and allows risks to go unnoticed.

- Avoiding interpersonal conflicts hampers teamwork. Managers who fail to deal with team members who have insufficient skills or destructive behaviors set up a conflict debt that affects every member of the team.

- Conflict debt is deeply personal, too. When you fail to advocate for a manageable workload, an investment in your career development, or even basic working conditions that suit you, you allow work to become a significant source of stress.

CONFLICT AVERSION
AND AVOIDANCE

I AM AS CONFLICT averse as they come. Really.

It's not lost on me that I am a professional conflict instigator. I assure you that my profession notwithstanding, I get sweaty palms and mild nausea at the thought of getting into a disagreement when I'm outside the comfortable confines of a client's boardroom, where I feel in control. To be honest, it doesn't even have to be a disagreement—I feel uncomfortable when I think that something I did will cause someone, almost anyone, to dislike me.

An aversion to conflict was baked into me from my earliest days. I was raised in a beautiful home with a loving family. We gathered each night to have dinner and watch *The MacNeil/Lehrer Report* on PBS. Discussion was encouraged. Debate was relished. Facts were questioned. There was only one rule: anything that could be classified as fighting was verboten. I can't recall a single instance when either of my parents raised their voice at me or each other. Not once.

I suspect that my father was at the root of the issue. My mother is a strong, confident person who has never been shy to stand up for what she believes in; my dad was different. He was sensitive and attuned to the power of language. He used words to lift people up and was careful never to use them as weapons. As an example, my friends were always taken aback at our house because profanity was allowed, and sometimes even encouraged. There were only two forbidden terms in our house: "shut up" and "stupid," because those were aimed at other people. In our house, "shit" was not a bad word.

I believe that my dad's unwillingness to inflict conflict on others was tied to the profound effect it had on him. When people hurt my dad, the wound never closed. I recall situations where the damage from the most minor incidents persisted years after the original transgression. Of course, his sensitivity affected the rest of the family. We learned not to broach uncomfortable topics. We had to watch, listen, and infer what one another liked and didn't like with keen sleuthing. It once took me two years to draw my dad out of a funk. I finally wrangled it out of him that he was worried I wouldn't take care of my mother when he was gone. He brooded about it but didn't say a word. He was impressively conflict averse.

What Is Conflict Aversion?

Conflict aversion is a general unease with the idea of getting into a disagreement. It often starts as a kid at the dinner table and follows you all the way to the boardroom table. You might have a mild form of conflict aversion, which you are able to overcome with a deep breath and some bolstering self-talk: "You got this!" Or you might have such a strong distaste for conflict that you avoid or withdraw from any situation with even the slightest risk that an argument might erupt. The stronger your conflict aversion, the more debilitating it becomes. As we discussed in Chapter 1, organizations require conflict; avoiding it just creates conflict debt.

Where Does Conflict Aversion Come From?

Our distaste for conflict comes from many different sources; both nature and nurture are causes. Recognizing how conflict debt has built up over your lifetime is the first step to understanding how conflict aversion is affecting your work and your life. Let's look at the different influences that might make you uncomfortable about being uncomfortable.

Our Wiring

We come into the world conflict averse. Humans have evolved that way because conflict is hard on relationships, and relationships are key to survival. Our cave-dwelling ancestors didn't want to get into a fight that would have them shoved out of the cave and left to the saber-toothed tiger. Genetically and physiologically, you aren't that far removed from your prehistoric predecessors. Your brain is constantly scanning for threats to your safety and when it recognizes one, it steers you away. Today, those threats seldom include saber-toothed tigers, but they are still closely linked to losing your place in the tribe and being voted out of the cave. I won't belabor this point. It's enough to recognize that your conflict aversion is partly biological.

Childhood

You arrive in the world wired to seek connection and avoid conflict, and it doesn't take long before your parents and role models reinforce that predisposition. Much of your conflict aversion can be traced back to lessons you were taught as a kid. Back then, these lessons went under the heading of "good manners." Twentieth-century parents saw conflict as antithetical to politeness. The general idea was that conflict is undignified, but the adults around you had their own clichés and catchphrases to get the point across. Here are four of my favorites.

1. "If you can't say anything nice, don't say anything at all."

If you had a grandparent who said this, they were probably trying to teach you not to be mean. For the record, I agree with Grandma that you shouldn't have called Freddie's bike a "sissy bike" just because it had a basket and handlebar streamers. But when your mom asked if you liked your lunch and Grandma chastised you for telling her that the pear she packed was bruised and inedible by the time it got to school, I start to take issue with dear old Grandma.

The problem is that Grandma was teaching you that it's better for everything to *look* good on the surface than for it to actually *be* good. It didn't matter whether you liked your lunch or not, you were supposed to spare your mother's feelings and say it was "good." Saving face for all involved was a hallmark of getting along in polite society. So, you stifled your concerns and learned that it's more important that other people feel good than that you do.

Once you internalize that lesson, it shows up in so many ways in your adult life. Now the bruised pear in your lunch is an undercooked piece of chicken at a restaurant. When the waiter enquires about your meal, you smile and tell him that it's "fine." You choke down the outer bit, hide the jiggly pink middle part under the mashed potatoes, and hope you don't spend the night calling Ralph on the big porcelain phone. If you follow Grandma's Not Nice Rule, you endure the miserable experience and never speak of it again.

Unfortunately, you probably put your own spin on the Not Nice Rule at some point. It morphed into Not Nice Rule B: "If you can't say anything nice, wait 'til you're out of earshot." You switched to that because you learned that stifling your negative comment doesn't erase your negative thought. You needed to vent your unhealthy emotions somewhere, so you found a safer outlet. If you've adopted this passive-aggressive form of the Not Nice Rule, the day after your chicken fiasco, you tell four friends about the terrible experience and post a one-star review on Yelp. You inflict all this damage without ever giving the waiter or the restaurant the chance to make it right. Grandma should be feeling sheepish right about now!

The Not Nice Rule wreaks havoc at work, too. The jiggly pink chicken is now your teammate's presentation, with a central tenet as undercooked as your poultry. You say nothing in the meeting and either let the presentation go forward without the benefit of some constructive feedback or, worse, you go with option B and whisper to your colleagues about the ridiculous presentation in the hallway afterward.

2. "Mind your own business."

Grandma's isn't the only voice in your head encouraging your conflict aversion. Somewhere along the way, you might have had a teacher who told you to "mind your own business." In my case, it was my fourth grade teacher, Mrs. Rankin, who used to say, "Mind your own beeswax." I never did understand where that expression came from or how harmonious hive behavior related to fourth grade. What I do know is that it meant I was supposed to watch in silence as conversations and relationships around me deteriorated. My classmates' bad behavior could range from excluding unpopular kids to stealing baseball cards. In all cases, the expectation was to mind my own business and if I broke that rule, I was the "tattletale."

The problem with the Mind Your Own Business Rule is that you learn to put up with behavior that takes a huge toll on you. I suffered with my classmates' dysfunctional dynamics because, even though these dynamics impacted my experiences on the playground, in the classroom, and for forty minutes a day on the school bus, apparently they weren't technically "my business."

The damage inflicted went beyond you, too. No one taught you how to discern if your friends' roughhousing was healthy and therefore covered by the rule, or if it was bullying and therefore exempt. Maybe it was both. Their tussle started as roughhousing, so you stayed out of it only to watch as it devolved into something more dangerous. How much bullying did you witness silently from the sidelines? One review of bullying research concluded that in 85% of all bullying episodes, one or more bystanders witness the mistreatment. In only 10% of these situations does the bystander intervene.[6] This statistic is all the more disturbing when you learn that when a bystander speaks up, the majority of incidents end within ten seconds. Do we really want kids to "mind their own business"?

Not all of the bad behavior you witness at work is as horrible as bullying. Some is more innocuous but damaging nonetheless.

It might be as simple as ignoring your colleagues' obvious misalignment on an issue. The issue will pop up later as the gap becomes a major chasm during implementation. The ensuing back and forth slows everything down and also creates animosity that could have been rectified if you'd asked the parties to clarify their positions at the beginning.

Other instances of bad behavior can be more toxic. For example, you might learn about rifts on your team by becoming the outlet for your colleagues' venting and gossip. You hear them question one another's competence or even their integrity, but you don't know what to do. You just let them vent, not knowing how to be helpful or to diffuse their anger and frustration. You stay on the sidelines because, after all, it's none of your business.

3. "*Now* look what you've done!"

Do you remember what happened when you were young and another kid started to cry or throw a temper tantrum in response to something you said? If you had an experience like mine, an adult appeared out of thin air, hands on hips, finger wagging to admonish you with "*Now* look what you've done!" It wasn't always clear what your transgression was, but you were 100% clear that you were in trouble.

You likely learned two things in that "Now look what you've done" moment. First, other people's emotions are bad and public displays of emotion are to be avoided. At least that's what you logically concluded because every time someone expressed anger, sadness, or frustration, the adults spiraled in different ways. The nurturing types tried to quickly placate the emotional child with reassurances or a lollipop. The purveyors of tough love responded with an emotional outburst of their own: "*You kids are driving me mental!*"

Second, you learned that you were to blame for the other kid's emotions. Maybe all you said to Sam was that you weren't free for a playdate because you got invited to Jordan's birthday party. Sam felt excluded and burst into tears, but you hadn't said anything malicious. How were you supposed to know that Sam wasn't invited to the party? Adults don't care about the backstory. They arrive on scene, triage who is crying, and immediately blame the other person. Sam is emotional, but you're at fault.

Now as an adult, you're tiptoeing around any issue that might upset someone. Your team has serious issues to work through, but you're convinced that the terrain is riddled with emotional land mines and you are not going to risk detonating one. Rather than wander into unsafe territory, you just let it go. As a result, the criers and yellers have your team held hostage. You can't go through it, so you go around it. No way you are going to take the blame for unleashing tears in a meeting.

4. "Stay out of trouble."

Our unhealthy relationship with power starts in childhood, too. When your teachers, coaches, or Scout troop leaders were mean, unfair, or ineffective, your complaints fell on deaf ears. You were told to "stay out of trouble," like the time you came home from soccer practice to report a great injustice perpetrated by the coach, only to get a pat on the head with a "try harder" and a "be good."

You learned not to question people in positions of power. You learned that might is right. You learned that when someone senior to you does something you don't like, it's you who has to change, not them. You learn to tough it out, rather than say something that might expose the person in power to the error of their ways.

It's no surprise that as an adult, you are hesitant to say anything that might question or challenge your superiors. After all, if you say something, you might "get into trouble." Instead, you let your destructive, disorganized, or even dishonest boss go on inflicting damage because you don't want to upset her... and you definitely don't want to get fired. You know to tough it out rather than trying to make it better.

One caveat: although the Stay Out of Trouble Rule was likely true for you as a child, my experience with my own children's cohort tells me that this rule is evolving. Today's so-called helicopter parents are not as likely to defer to authority figures, particularly when it comes to their precious children. Unfortunately, these overprotective parents haven't taught their children how to speak truth to power; instead, the parents themselves come to their children's rescue to take on the teacher, principal, or coach. This "rescuing" just teaches kids that power (teacher) must be fought with power (parent). Sadly, the end result is still a strong inclination toward conflict aversion. I'll speak more about the damage we're doing in raising conflict-avoidant children in the Bonus Chapter.

More Sinister Causes of Conflict Aversion

Up to this point, I've been talking about the misguided but well-intentioned ways the adults in our lives taught us that conflict is impolite. Of course, there are many more sinister situations that might have contributed to your conflict aversion. I have met several people recently, predominantly women, who were told repeatedly as children, in more and less direct ways, to stifle their voices. Some of them quite literally: "You're *too* loud!" Others with various subtle cues: shushes, or admonishments that children are meant to be seen and not heard. If you were raised by someone who denied you your voice, it's not your fault that speaking your mind feels wrong.

Being silenced or ignored is not the worst cause of conflict aversion. If you grew up in a household where arguments were nasty, hurtful, or even violent, your fear of conflict is completely justified. For you, conflict can't be productive; it can only be harmful. You learned to keep everything harmonious and to avoid igniting an argument. You became adept at maneuvering without setting anyone off. Lacking a role model for healthy conflict, you never learned that such a thing exists. Avoiding conflict at all costs was a logical and rational response to the world you lived in. I assure you, there is an alternative.

Beyond the Home

As you got older, your views about conflict started to be shaped by people outside your home. In adolescence, your peers became a significant influence. If your high school friends were like mine, they didn't take too kindly to you questioning their actions. Saying that you didn't want to drink or smoke seemed rational to you, but to your friends, it was decidedly uncool. You learned that if you want to be in the in-crowd, you should keep your divergent thoughts to yourself.

There is compelling evidence that people will go to great lengths to avoid being the lone dissenting voice in a group. The most famous of these studies was the 1955 Solomon Asch experiment.[7] In the study, researchers presented a roomful of students with a series of lines. The lines were of noticeably different lengths. When Asch paid all but one of the students to say the shorter line was the longer line, the outlier eventually acquiesced and said that the short line was the longest. The power to fit in with the group is profound.

Some days at work it probably feels like you're a participant in your very own Asch experiment. "Are we looking at the same lines?" For me, it was within two months of starting my first job that I got the message loud and clear: go along to get along. I had been hired out of graduate school to analyze employee surveys in a consulting firm. I worked alongside a colleague who was much more tenured than me. He had been doing all the statistics before I came on board. On the very first project we worked on together, it became clear to me that he had made errors in his analysis. His conclusions were incorrect and misleading. I did what I had been taught in school: I calmly and directly pointed out the errors. My main focus was the implications of sharing indefensible conclusions with our clients. In my mind, I was saving the day. Unfortunately, his boss thought I was out of line and communicated her displeasure to my manager. I hadn't been *nice*. I wasn't even halfway through my first notepad as a working woman and I had already learned to keep my mouth shut.

This conflict-avoidant boss was teaching me to be conflict avoidant, too. This phenomenon is backed up by research that has shown that conflict-avoidant bosses beget conflict-avoidant subordinates. A study by Michele Gelfand and her colleagues demonstrated that the conflict style of the leader translated into what they called the "conflict culture" of the unit.[8] Managers who avoided conflict led units that avoided conflict.

☰ CONFLICT ☰
IS A NATURAL PART OF
• HEALTHY •
RELATIONSHIPS
AND A CRITICAL
›DEFENSE‹
AGAINST UNHEALTHY ONES.

If you've worked in a conflict-avoidant culture, you know exactly what it looks like. It starts with managers eschewing arguments, but it snowballs from there. Soon, your organization is rolling out the new organizational values with "teamwork" and "mutual respect" prominent among them. As you walk past the values plaque on the wall, you scoff when you notice the word "integrity" at the top of the list. Clearly integrity doesn't mean saying what you believe if what you believe might disrupt the harmonious teamwork.

I mentioned that I used to work in a firm that did employee surveys. I have significant guilt about the role that employee surveys have played in perpetuating conflict aversion. It all seemed so innocuous and well intentioned at the time, but somewhere along the way, the employee engagement trend became synonymous with keeping everyone happy. We taught managers not to rock the boat and not to make anyone too uncomfortable. To make sure they got the message, we tied their employees' ratings to their bonuses. Now we expect managers to accentuate accountability, champion change, and transform the transformation, but for goodness' sake, make sure you keep everyone happy!

Your parents taught you that people with good manners don't have uncomfortable conversations. They taught you to zip it, look away, or back down. Next, your teachers, coaches, and bosses piled on to make good and sure that you would keep your concerns to yourself or at least raise them in the gentlest fashion. You still hear all their voices in your head when you even contemplate saying something that might cause friction. My friend calls her voices the "Itty-Bitty Shitty Committee." You know the ones: they sit on your shoulder and whisper bad advice in your ear.

Thanks to the Itty-Bitty Shitty Committee, you learned to avoid conflict. And because conflict wasn't allowed, you never learned how to have conflict openly, kindly, or productively. Now you don't know how to use conflict as a natural part of healthy relationships or as a critical defense against unhealthy ones. No wonder you're in conflict debt.

Conflict aversion is what leads to conflict debt. When your leaders don't want to have conflict, they don't prioritize. So now you're doing a little bit of everything without sufficient resources to do any-thing properly. That's why everyone has eighty-seven things on their to-do lists and thirty-two hours of meetings a week. On top of that, because your manager doesn't like conflict, she doesn't do anything when your teammates' behavior in those meetings is atrocious, so thirty-one of the thirty-two hours of meetings you have each week are excruciatingly painful. And because you were taught not to like conflict, you don't advocate to make it any better.

Conflict Aversion versus Conflict Avoidance

I told you from the start that I am conflict averse. I worry and rumi-nate about uncomfortable conversations just like you do. So how does a person who has been conflict averse since birth end up in a career where she has to unearth conflicts every day? I have spent more than two decades witnessing firsthand the cost of conflict debt on organizations, teams, and individuals. One day, I finally decided that I didn't want to let my conflict aversion rule me. (It was a bit like the day I decided to stop drinking soda.) It turns out that conflict aversion isn't really the problem: conflict avoidance is the problem.

What's the difference between conflict aversion and conflict avoidance? Conflict aversion means that you don't like conflict. You are wary of it and would prefer a day without it. Conflict avoidance means that you don't have conflict. You actively sidestep situations that require you to disagree with others. Conflict aversion doesn't hurt you until it changes into conflict avoidance. Unfortunately, you might not yet differentiate between the two. You just know that you don't like conflict, but you don't think about the option of engaging in it anyway.

Maybe this will help. I think about my conflict avoidance exactly the same way I think about exercise. I really don't enjoy exercising. I am not one of those people who loves to get sweaty, who joneses for the endorphin rush. Nope. I am exercise averse. But I exercise. I pull on the most figure-flattering Lycra I can find, and I tough it out for an hour a few times a week. I don't let my exercise aversion turn into exercise avoidance. My health isn't negatively affected by my exercise aversion; it would only be affected if I let that aversion turn into exercise avoidance.

Conflict Avoidance

Researchers who study conflict classify it into different scenarios. One prominent conflict model, the Thomas–Kilmann Instrument, uses two dimensions: whether your approach meets *your* needs (which they call "assertive") and whether it meets *the other party's* needs (which they call "cooperative"). The model can be understood as four boxes, as follows: working to meet both party's needs is "collaborating"; meeting your own needs without regard for the other person's is "competing"; meeting the other party's needs without getting your own needs met is "accommodating"; and not attempting to meet anyone's needs is "avoiding." In the middle of the grid lies "compromising," where both parties are trying to meet at least some of the other's needs.

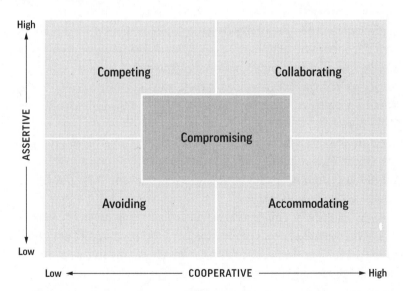

In this model, two conflict modes can be labeled conflict avoidant. The most conflict-avoidant strategy, as you would expect, is avoidance. In this scenario, you completely circumvent the topic and provide no opportunity for you or the other person to work toward a solution. You employ an avoidance strategy when you change the subject, skip the meeting, or duck into the bathroom to evade the person in question. Avoidance creates no forum for getting the issue on the table, let alone getting it resolved.

For conflict-averse people, avoidance can be a double-edged sword. Although you're deferring the unpleasantness for a while, you might be allowing the pressure to build. Depending on the importance of the issue and the personality of the person involved, this might cause an eruption, leading to an unpleasant encounter where the conflict is much more extreme than it would have been if you'd addressed the issue up front. That makes it seem like there are only two options: avoiding conflict or engaging in ugly conflict. In that way, your conflict avoidance leads to greater conflict aversion, and the vicious cycle continues.

A slightly less severe mode of conflict avoidance is one where you engage (or can't escape) the uncomfortable topic, but you take a passive approach: you "accommodate." In the accommodating scenario, you let the other party have their needs met without lobbying to meet your own, akin to dropping the rope in a tug-of-war: "I give up, you win." In doing so, you haven't avoided the issue, but you have avoided the conflict. If you cede your ground without a fight, you do nothing to meet your needs or the needs of the people who were counting on you. You might be letting down the rest of your team or missing a chance to make the idea work better or giving up an opportunity to point out a flaw in the plan. There is a price to pay for obliging, and it's paid by you and everyone who was counting on you to get your point across.

The final conflict mode that is worth discussing under the heading of conflict avoidance is compromising. Compromising isn't always conflict avoidant, but sliding into the quickest available solution that doesn't fully meet either of your needs suggests conflict-avoidant people trying to get out of the uncomfortable situation as quickly as possible.

In his excellent book *Never Split the Difference*, FBI hostage negotiator and conflict expert Chris Voss illustrates the effects of compromise. He imagines a situation where a husband wants to wear black shoes while his wife wants him to wear brown shoes. The compromise is to wear one black and one brown, a wholly inadequate solution. When I hear two people compromising with the express purpose of getting out of the uncomfortable conversation as quickly as possible, I picture them each wearing one black and one brown shoe—someone call the fashion police.

I am not saying that conflict avoidance is universally bad. The Thomas–Kilmann theory is based on the idea that each conflict mode has a time and place. There are situations where it makes sense to avoid the issue. For example, when everyone is too emotional to handle the discussion constructively, it can be wise to postpone it for a while. There are situations where obliging is the optimal approach, particularly if the issue is very important to the other person and not as important to you. Of course, there are situations where compromising is the way to go. Not when it means leaving the house in two different-colored shoes, but when there really is no solution that completely meets both party's needs and the middle ground optimizes the outcome for everyone. Like, oh, I don't know, if our politicians used a little more compromise to keep the trains running, take care of those in need, and keep us out of World War III. Just a thought.

I'm not suggesting that you worry if you employ the avoiding, obliging, or compromising strategies deliberately and occasionally. You do need to worry when these become your default conflict modes. That's when your conflict avoidance affects your ability to effectively advocate for the issues and the people you're responsible for. It's natural for you to be conflict averse; it's harmful if you allow yourself to become conflict avoidant.

In Brief

- Conflict aversion is a general unease with the thought of getting into a disagreement. It starts when you're young and can stay with you for your whole life.

- As humans, we're wired to dislike conflict, having evolved to get along with others as a means of staying safe.

- As children, we were encouraged by influential adults to avoid conflict because being disagreeable was considered bad manners.

- In the workforce, we are encouraged to go along to get along. Those who violate this norm are often given critical feedback and labeled as poor team players.

- Conflict is a natural part of healthy relationships and a critical defense against unhealthy ones.

- While conflict aversion is normal, it's important that it not turn into conflict avoidance. Disliking conflict will not hurt us, but disavowing it will.

3

A NEW CONFLICT
MINDSET

I **AM SITTING IN** a senior executive's office at a Fortune 500 company. He is surrounded by several members of his support team. We're meeting to plan a session I will facilitate for his executives. They want to have really candid conversations and they think having a facilitator will help. I've worked with the organization before and they know that's exactly my sweet spot—helping teams wade into treacherous conversations.

As we begin, I can't help but notice our surroundings. The executive's office is modern and practical—no vestiges of the old executive row with the giant mahogany desks. Instead, we're all seated around a table looking very casual and comfortable. But underneath, no one is quite as relaxed as it seems. The support team is anxious. They need this meeting to go well.

The discussion starts off well. The leader provides some context and shares his vision for the session. As we get deeper into the discussion, it's all starting to sound a bit safe. I'm disturbed by the leader's description of his organization, which paints a rosier picture than what I've witnessed in the other projects in which I've been involved at the organization. Given that I've been brought in to generate candid conversations, I'm quick to share my contradictory assessment.

The executive flinches but then diverts the conversation back to more mundane matters. I register the offense but think little of it. I reassure (or delude) myself that it's my edgy style that makes me valuable. We get the meeting back on track and I close by reiterating the executive's objectives and committing to next steps.

What's interesting is what happens next. Apparently, what I saw as a little hiccup, others see as a bigger concern. The entire support team is nervous about how the meeting went. It's obvious to them that I've offended the executive and they think there will be fallout. There are whispers about whether the session will proceed, or at least whether it will proceed with me.

What would you do as one of the supporting players in this scenario? Your boss was clearly taken aback but didn't say anything. You don't know how he's processing the conversation or what impact it will have on your project. The consultant is vulnerable because of her misstep, but she's also a bit overpowering and you're not sure how she would react to you questioning her approach. Do you say something? To whom?

My first clue that my comments might have actually been a transgression comes in an email I receive from one of the project leads. In it, he simply asks, "How do you think that went?" Gulp. Very few people ask, "How do you think that went?" when they think it went great. He suggests we get on a call to discuss it. The call is similarly cryptic. It opens with a few pleasantries from the project team members and then the lead asks me, "So, how do you think that went?" I pause. It's clear that I'm not going to get any feedback until I give my assessment. Are they hoping I will confess that I blew it, which will save them from having to say anything awkward?

To be fair, by asking this question, the project team member is doing more to help me than the folks who are keeping quiet. At least his question has tipped me off that there's something I should be worried about. That's much more helpful than the people who are saying nothing. I eventually answer the question by saying that the meeting achieved what we needed it to achieve, but that I am concerned with the leader's response to my comments. That still doesn't inspire candor from the team. By the end of the call, I'm not much clearer on what really transpired and what I need to do differently, but I am clear that I will be much more careful from now on.

What really helps me get my head on straight is when one of the members of the team calls me privately the next day. She is clear, kind, and candid about how my behavior impacted the executive and might affect the project. She starts by telling me that she wants to make sure this project is successful. She shares her feedback on how my comments might have landed and works with me to figure out what to do next. I am grateful. She tells me what I need to hear and leaves me with not only greater confidence in how to proceed on the project but also the sense that I have a great ally.

What caused the members of this project team to behave so differently? I believe their behavior was attributable to their individual mindsets about conflict. A person who believes that conflict is unpleasant and unhealthy will say nothing. A person who believes conflict is important but distasteful will hint at the underlying issue and hope their point lands. A person who believes conflict leads to better understanding and better outcomes will directly and matter-of-factly raise the issue. Fortunately, dealing with this situation early in the project gave me an opportunity to encourage them to be straight with me. For the rest of the project, everyone gave me the honest feedback I needed to make sure we were successful.

The Case against Conflict

There are so many stories you can conjure if you want to let yourself off the hook in an uncomfortable situation. Remember the Itty-Bitty Shitty Committee is whispering all those excuses in your ear all the time: "Don't say anything that isn't nice," "That's none of your business," "What if she gets angry and turns it back on you?" and the kicker, "You can't say that, you'll get fired!" As long as you listen to them, you'll never address the issue. No one wants to be mean, nosy, or unemployed.

The only way you will approach these difficult situations is if you adopt a new mindset—one in which you accept that working through conflict is good for everyone. You need to replace the naysaying voices with supportive, encouraging ones who are talking you into doing the right thing, not talking you out of it. It's time to dispatch the members of the Itty-Bitty Shitty Committee, one by one.

Kind Is the New Nice

Let's start with Committee Member #1: Grandma. I'm not suggesting that Grandma was wrong when she encouraged you to be nice. I like being nice and prefer when others are nice to me. It's nice when someone grabs the door when my hands are full. It's nice if you compliment me when you think my idea is cool. Saying or doing something positive is nice. The problem is when you use the excuse of being nice to *avoid* doing or saying something *constructive*. Then you're using nice to avoid conflicts that would actually be kind.

In the example with the fallout from the Fortune 500 executive meeting above, I truly believe that the people who kept quiet and didn't share their concerns were trying to be nice. Telling me that I had screwed up would have questioned my ability (or at least my judgment). It might have upset me to realize I had messed up in front of such an important client. It could have made me nervous about the prospect of losing the contract. It definitely wouldn't have felt nice.

But making nice in the moment wouldn't have been kind in the long run. If no one had told me the impact my comments had on the executive, I might have gone into the next meeting and been equally forthright. Without shifting my approach, I could have found myself booted out for insubordination. That would have meant the loss of a very important project for me. It's better to be kind than to be nice.

Apply the nice versus kind filter to other mission-critical conflicts in your organization. Imagine you are one of the people deciding which projects get fully funded and which will be nixed or forced to struggle along under-resourced. You know how hard everyone has been working and don't want to discourage them. Is it better to stop the project after three months of hard work or kill it after they've invested nine?

While doing my dissertation research, I met a team that paid the price for others' desires to be nice. The team spent fourteen years building an innovative new product. Although it was a great idea at the outset, the company strategy had shifted, and it was no longer a good fit. That made it a low priority for funding. Each funding cycle, the team would receive mediocre feedback and just enough money to allow them to hobble along for another year. No one had the guts to tell them the project didn't have a future. Desperate for the money to accelerate the project, they chose a radical strategy. While the CEO was visiting their location, they would hijack his limousine and set up a product demo inside. You've gotta give them credit for chutzpah.

Unfortunately, the story doesn't have a happy ending. Rather than heralding the amazing new product, the CEO killed it. All those people trying to be nice led to this team embarrassing themselves in front of the CEO—definitely not kind. Fourteen years of work and millions of dollars went down the drain. You won't be surprised to learn that this very large organization eventually went bankrupt. This example is a good reminder that there is a real financial cost of using nice as an excuse for conflict avoidance.

Think of the cost of being nice in your organization. If you don't want to say something mean, you're going to struggle to shelve a product line that someone has worked hard to build. If you only want to say things that are nice, you're not going to tell the head of supply chain that she hasn't done enough to bring your costs down. If you don't want to cause discomfort, you definitely won't tell the product guys that their new design isn't what your customers were asking for.

If you're too focused on being nice, you're not focused enough on being kind, being profitable, being innovative, or being around five years from now.

Next time you hear Grandma telling you that what you're about to say isn't nice, ask yourself:

1. Will what I have to say make the person aware of something they are better off knowing?
2. Will saying something uncomfortable now help the person avoid a more adverse situation in the future?
3. Is making a tough call now better for our business in the long run?

It's kind to say something uncomfortable in the moment that will make things better in the long run. It's a version of nice that is beyond politeness and face-saving, and closer to benevolence. It's a version of nice that puts the onus on you to ignore a little discomfort or embarrassment in favor of making everyone more successful.

Get Off the Sidelines

The second concern we have to deal with if you're going to start working through conflict constructively is the fear of sticking your nose where it doesn't belong. As Committee Member #2, Teacher, taught us, "minding your own business" is easier, safer, and arguably politer than wading in where you weren't invited. There had better be a good rationale for getting involved in something messy that you could otherwise have avoided. I assure you, there is.

The best rationale for getting involved in something that seems like none of your business is that it probably is your business. Let's try a test. Think of a disruptive, unproductive, unhealthy situation you've been witnessing at work. Now, answer the following questions. Do the people involved have the same company name on their business card? Does their behavior affect your customers, suppliers, or partners? Do the shenanigans you're trying to ignore impact your ability to get your job done effectively and efficiently? If you answered "yes" to even one of those questions, I'd argue that it is your business.

It's your business when there's a disagreement between two teams about how to design a process you'll have to implement. It's your business which project to prioritize and which to delay. Don't forget the obvious issues either: the never-ending squabble between two of your teammates; the incessant complaining about the new receptionist; and your boss's tendency to give your coworkers all the high-profile tasks. These are all your business. Any unresolved issue that affects your work, your customers, or your organization is your business and might just be an opportunity for you to add value.

Although it's easy to conclude that your involvement is not invited nor welcomed, the more important question is whether or not it would be valuable. Here's a different way of thinking of your role as a witness to conflict debt. If two or more of your colleagues are mired in a conflict, it's likely they won't be able to get themselves out of it, at least not quickly. Each side has become entrenched and only sees the situation from their own biased point of view. The discussion ceases to be rational and becomes highly emotional. Once it reaches this point, it's unlikely that this conflict will resolve without outside help. That's where you have something very important to offer as the witness: greater objectivity and more emotional distance. That makes it easier for you to see a potential solution than it is for the people who are in the thick of it. You have a better vantage point from which to unlock the solution than the parties to the disagreement.

I remember one team where this was particularly true. It was an executive team in the food business. The team was directed by a razor-sharp leader named Matt. When I say "razor-sharp," I mean both in intellect and communication style. You didn't want to be in an argument with Matt, but it seemed that someone was always on his bad side. In one weekly management meeting, Matt chose to pick on Steve, the head of sales. He peppered Steve with questions about his numbers, pushing him for justification but leaving little room for him to get a word in edgewise. Matt wanted to know why the sales numbers for some products were down. He was drilling into specific products, extracting any numbers that supported his concerns. Steve was in trouble. No approach he took would placate Matt. If he backed down and admitted he didn't know why the numbers were down, it would incite more anger—Matt hated weakness and lack of accountability. If Steve kept standing up for himself, it would prolong the unwinnable tug-of-war with his boss.

Enter Russell, the master of healthy conflict. He had been listening and watching, waiting for the right moment to defuse the argument. Although Russell worked in operations, he was a savvy businessperson and could follow the conversation and see the holes in Matt's logic. He didn't wait for a lull, he just spoke calmly and quietly over Matt: "It looks like the decline in traditional product might have to do with a volume shift toward the organic option last week." Everyone looked up. Russell knew that he didn't have to solve the problem; he just needed to offer a path forward. "Steve, would it make sense to get a little more information on whether this is a one-time issue due to our organic promotion or if it's an actual trend?" The tenor changed instantly. It was as though the leader had become so myopically focused on the target of his wrath that he had lost sight of the dozen witnesses around the table. Russell's contribution had caused Matt to release his grip. The conversation was now about understanding instead of blaming. It was about what to do next, not what had already happened. It was no longer conflict but problem-solving. Russell could have easily played the spectator like his colleagues around the table, but his timely intervention steered the conversation in a much more fruitful direction. Steve could catch his breath and come back with a good answer to Matt's challenge.

Russell is not typical. Our first human instinct is to protect ourselves, not to run headfirst into danger. If the conflict on your team starts to take on a more sinister tone, you need to think about your obligation to step up. When I think about the #MeToo movement and how people such as Harvey Weinstein, Bill O'Reilly, or Kevin Spacey abused their power, it's the witnesses' roles that distress me most. Sadly, I'm not surprised that there are wicked people in the world who abuse their power. I understand why those who have been

YOUR REFUSAL TO BE A
➤ **BYSTANDER,** ◄
BOTH TO MINOR SCUFFLES
AND MAJOR
▪ **INJUSTICES,** ▪
WILL MAKE YOUR
≡ **ORGANIZATION** ≡
BETTER.

wounded and victimized stay silent. But thinking about the assistants and HR professionals and board members who sat idly by as powerful men preyed on the powerless deeply saddens me.

Next time you hear that teacher's voice inside your head telling you to "mind your own business," answer these questions:

1. Would my intervening help to balance a situation with a power gap?
2. Could I use my credibility or influence to make the situation better?
3. Do I have a perspective on the issue that will help open up potential solutions?

Being willing to wade into a difficult situation that doesn't directly involve you takes guts. It requires you to think beyond the normal rules of engagement and to see a role in conflict for the person who has traditionally been only a witness. Getting involved doesn't mean you're overstepping; it means you have a greater sense of ownership for the success of your team and your organization. Your refusal to be a bystander, both to minor scuffles and major injustices, will make your organization better.

Work through the Emotion

Itty-Bitty Shitty Committee Member #3 that we need to dismiss is the one who's afraid of emotional outbursts. How are you supposed to proactively address conflict if you are tiptoeing around to avoid upsetting people? The emotional types have you held hostage. Don't be fooled: it seems like avoiding the conflict will result in less drama, but it won't. If frustration, anger, sadness, guilt, or envy lie beneath the surface, those emotions will continue to quietly affect your team and your organization until they are exhumed and addressed. The fastest way to the other side of the conflict is through the emotions, not around them.

Take Monica, an executive in a global high-tech product company. I facilitated a session with Monica and her five male colleagues—

including her boss, the CEO. We were well into a very normal strategic discussion when, unexpectedly, Monica started to cry. The men shifted uncomfortably in their seats and dropped eye contact, hoping that I would *deal with it*. Isn't that why you hire a facilitator, so they will deal with the messy stuff?

Rewind ten minutes. We had been discussing the growth of the company and their plans. All the talk was focused on the small newly acquired business unit, rather than on the large mature unit that Monica leads. When one of her colleagues asked her to weigh in on the strategy, Monica finally took the floor. Her colleague had given her the chance to express her anger. "My business unit is four times the size of Hans's and it's responsible for an even greater proportion of the profit, but my team gets hardly any of your attention. The majority of R&D money is going to Hans, not to mention that the last three acquisitions all landed there as well. What am I supposed to tell my people?" Monica had been talking about what her team needed to keep growing, and no one had been listening. Most days she would have the energy to keep asking calmly and politely but now she was exhausted from flying all over the world to see customers, and when her teammate asked about what her unit needs, the tears started to flow.

We didn't stop the meeting. We didn't even take a break. No one pulled the fire alarm. I simply said to Monica, "Okay, this is important." I encouraged her teammates to calmly, rationally, and kindly ask a few questions to get at the unresolved issue. We treated Monica's emotions and her values as just another data set, as valid and important as any facts or information that we could be discussing. By keeping the intensity as low as possible, Monica got through the emotion. The tears didn't last long, and she was soon back to the measured, pragmatic, tough senior executive we were all used to.

It turns out that the team being willing to explore how Monica was feeling was the best thing that could have happened. The CEO admitted in front of the whole team that he'd been on a dangerous path of over-investing in the sexy new unit and starving the business that was paying the bills. The whole team talked about how Monica's pleas had fallen on deaf ears for so long and how they could raise issues sooner next time. The emotion did its job: it signaled to everyone that something really important was going on under the surface.

An amazing study by Alex Pentland and his lab at MIT looked at hundreds of variables to see what actually predicts the performance of a team.[9] It turns out that one of the most important predictors of success on a wide variety of tasks is whether individuals are tuned in to the emotional states of their teammates. The collective *emotional intelligence* of the team predicted success while their collective *cognitive intelligence* did not. We used to talk about the emotionally sensitive person as the weakest link in the chain, but the research tells us they might just be the strongest.

If you're still struggling to see how emotions could have a place in the office, maybe this framing will help. I find it useful to think of unpleasant emotions similarly to how I think of pain. Neither is good for you in the long run, but they both serve a purpose in calling your attention to an underlying problem. The value of the emotional display is that it helps you identify that a conflict is present and gives you clues about its source. Both are tremendously valuable. Without exposing the emotional resistance, you risk letting it simmer, stalling decisions and threatening execution. Left untreated, it can do much more significant damage.

When you hear the voice inside your head chastising you for upsetting someone, ask yourself these questions:

1. Can we move forward effectively if there are issues that haven't been addressed or resolved?
2. Is this an important issue to discuss, regardless of how unpleasant the conversation might become?
3. Would I be better off if I understood how people are thinking and feeling about this issue?

It's time to stop seeing emotional displays as inappropriate at the office. Don't avoid conflicts for fear of triggering anger or tears. Old norms around decorum and professional demeanor aren't serving you anymore. Once you accept that emotions will always be part of work involving humans, you will recognize that it's better to address the emotions, rather than letting them quietly sabotage everything you're trying to accomplish.

Disagree with Your Boss

Committee Member #4: dear old Dad—constantly telling us to be good and stay out of trouble. As an adult, *trouble* means getting fired. I seldom make it through a week without someone telling me that taking my advice to put an issue on the table would make them lose their job. I am confident, based on years of working with managers at all levels, that these fears are greatly overstated. The fact that the fear has little basis in reality doesn't make it any less potent. If you're going to speak truth to power, you need a vision of how productive conflict will make you the *valued* employee, rather than the *former* employee.

One leader I worked with struggled to imagine a positive ending to a conflict with his boss. I was facilitating a session on leadership with the directors and vice presidents of a grocery chain. Their bosses, the executive team, wanted them to step up and take on more of the day-to-day management of the company so they could be freed up to focus on strategy. I started to hear grumblings in the room and got the sense that the leaders weren't buying it. Sure, the executives talk about staying out of the weeds, but they don't walk the talk.

One of the leaders, Pierre, gave me an example. "The role descriptions say that the category managers who report to me get to make the decisions about pricing, but just this week, one of the executives overrode my category manager and changed the price of a product." To Pierre, this was not only unfair to the category manager but also deeply embarrassing and emasculating for him. I suggested that he raise the issue with his boss. He looked me in the eye and said, "Yeah, right, I'd better dust off my résumé."

I don't think he really believed that. He was just frustrated. And my guess is that he was feeling crappy about not standing up to the executive and not backing up his employee. He just couldn't imagine how to raise the issue with his boss in a way that wouldn't create backlash. We worked through a few ideas about how to broach difficult conversations with your boss.

First, anchor your comments to something that matters to the business. In this case, the executives are on record saying that they need leaders at every level to step up so they can spend less time on the day-to-day and more time figuring out how they're going to battle Amazon. It's useful to refer to a business issue in your discussion to signal that the issue is important enough to justify a little discomfort. Pierre needed to mention the leadership project and how he and his colleagues were being asked to step up.

Second, stick to the facts. Instead of judging, be really precise with your language by objectively stating the behavior and outcome. It might *feel* like the boss has just humiliated you in front of one of your direct reports, but that's not how you want to broach the topic. Pierre didn't need to say anything more dramatic than "when you changed the price." There's no need for inflammatory language such as "when you overrode my decision."

Third, use the company language of values or principles to couch your comments. That way you're putting the discussion in the context of rules that everyone has agreed to. Pierre could refer to the company's value of integrity in explaining why he thought it was important to raise this issue when he was concerned about it.

Fourth, don't go in swinging. Disagreeing with the boss is *not* the moment to use your power poses. Nor is it the time for assertions or ultimatums. Evoke curiosity by using more questions than statements. That way, if your boss really doesn't like what you're saying, you leave yourself room to change your tack.

I suggested the following phrasing (names changed to protect the innocent): "I hear you that you think we got the price of pumpernickel wrong and that you want Penny to change it. I'm worried about overriding Penny's pumpernickel price at this point. I know you're trying to get everyone to step up and this might be a great learning experience for Penny. Would you be willing to let this one ride?"

Pierre's boss was working hard to show up differently and he took the feedback well. I know not all bosses would have responded so positively. Imagine the boss had erupted with "This isn't about pumpernickel, Pierre! It's about our margins and whether we have any hope at all of this company existing in two years! Don't you get that?!" That's when it's beneficial to have left your request open. You can respond with "I'm sorry. I was so focused on the development opportunity for Penny that I didn't think enough about the brand and the margin implications. I got it. I'll explain to Penny why it's the right thing to change the price."

Showing your boss that you've been listening to what he says, demonstrating that you care about your job enough to say something uncomfortable, and then being willing to defer to authority when the answer is "no" will raise your value in the eyes of most managers. You need to choose your spots wisely, but particularly when the issue is in the best interest of your company, it's better to raise the topic carefully than to leave it unresolved.

There are many great examples of issues where conflict with your boss is worth it. If your boss has not made her expectations clear to you, it's important to question her and understand the priorities. If you've been given a workload that you can't manage, it's better to discuss it than to struggle along. If you realize that you and a coworker received conflicting instructions, you need to clarify what was really expected. In each of these cases, having an uncomfortable conversation with your boss up front will reduce the likelihood of a much more unpleasant conversation later. If you don't address these issues, you might prioritize the wrong work and leave something important unfinished. If you don't surface an unmanageable workload, you risk the consequences for letting a ball drop. If you work at odds with a colleague, you will likely face the wrath when the misalignment is exposed down the line. Not every issue is worth challenging your boss over, but these and others trade minor discomfort now for major distress later.

If you are hearing a cautionary voice telling you to work hard and stay out of trouble, you can ask yourself these questions:

1. Do I need to do something different from what my boss instructed to be successful?
2. Will bringing up the issue now make it less likely that I'll face negative consequences later?
3. Would my colleagues thank me for having the courage to raise this issue?

I remember telling the CEO of a global bank that his employees feared telling him the truth for fear of being fired. He was completely perplexed. He kept asking, "Who? Who has ever been fired for asking a hard question?" He was keen to point out that the people who lose credibility in his eyes are the ones who shy away from the tough issues, not the ones who raise them.

It's time to decide which issues make the risk worth taking. Be smart and careful about how you wade into conflict with a superior. Start by linking to business issues and using questions to leave a back door open. Back down if you need to, but you'll be surprised how either now or later, your courage and willingness to stand up for what you believe in will be noticed and rewarded, both by your peers and your superiors. While there is a cost to challenging the status quo, there can be a higher cost of failing to act.

A New Mindset

Your organization is rife with issues that need to be actively addressed and resolved for the business to function effectively. If those discussions are ignored, postponed, or glossed over, the price of the conflict debt rises. I know that plodding into conflict is difficult; that's why you need a new mindset about conflict. Instead of viewing productive conflict as mean, upsetting, or risky, you need to see it as an opportunity to be kind, to be helpful, and to add value for your organization. That mindset will serve you and your company well over the long term.

One caveat. Each time I publish an article about adopting a constructive mindset for conflict, I get the odd comment about how my approach is "manipulative, condescending, and otherwise transparent and ineffective." I suspect if you felt the same way, you would already have used this book to line your hamster cage, but just in case, let me be explicit. All of the strategies for productive conflict in this book are based on the assumption that you *want* the conflict to be productive. If all you want is to win, or dominate, or ram your ideas down other people's throats regardless of the cost to your business or your relationships, then no, the techniques in this book are not for you.

The mindset for productive conflict is based on the idea that there is more than one version of the truth. It is underpinned by a genuine belief that diversity of thought leads to better outcomes. It is dependent on the assumption—borne out in research—that investing in getting everyone's position on the table will lead to not only higher quality decisions but better follow-through.[10]

The techniques you will read about in the following section do not assume that a productive mindset comes naturally, or even easily. As I discussed in Chapter 2, an enlightened mindset about conflict runs contrary to both nature and nurture, at least in the short term. But ultimately, it's exactly what you need to strengthen your business and your relationships.

In Brief

- Overcoming conflict avoidance requires a new mindset. We need to tune out the naysayers and focus on the positive outcomes that we'll achieve when we work through our conflicts.

- Although delivering difficult messages might not feel nice in the moment, in the long run, telling someone what they need to hear is often the kindest thing we can do.

- Rather than remaining a bystander to conflict, weigh in to help those in the thick of the argument solve their problem more objectively.

- Don't fear emotion; think of it as a valuable clue that something important is wrong. Calmly and kindly draw out the person to help rectify the underlying issues.

- Disagree with your boss when adding a different view will contribute to a better decision. Speak deliberately and respectfully, and leave a way to backtrack if necessary.

PART II
THE CONFLICT CODE

≋ INTRODUCTION ≋

IN CHAPTER 1, I shared how important productive conflict is to your organization. You saw how frequently conflict is required to set strategy, allocate resources, and prioritize activities. You learned that avoiding these conflicts creates a conflict debt that prevents your organization from making progress and also costs you significant personal interest in the form of frustration, disengagement, and burnout. I prepared you to start working through conflicts to avoid getting into debt again.

In Chapter 2, I admitted that paying off those conflicts as they emerge is easier said than done. Humans are wired for connection and we are hesitant to threaten our membership in the tribe. I took you down memory lane to help you realize how you became even more conflict averse as your parents, grandparents, teachers, and coaches all encouraged you to be nice and get along. You saw how those messages might have been reinforced when you entered the workforce. I warned you about letting your conflict aversion morph into full-blown conflict avoidance.

In Chapter 3, I made the case against conflict avoidance and argued that those voices in your head might be doing you a disservice. I showed you a few ways to beat them at their own game. I argued that conflict might not feel nice in the moment but that it's the kinder approach in the long run. I suggested that keeping out of other people's disagreements might be easier but being a witness to dysfunction just perpetuates it. I encouraged you to stop fearing emotional outbursts and start seeing them as the valuable clue that something important is wrong. I asked that we get over our fear of getting fired and start seeing the person who raises conflict as valuable, not dispensable. Those are the ideas that will help you develop a positive mindset about conflict.

In this section, we'll focus on what you can do to prevent the majority of conflicts and make the rest more productive and less aversive. You'll learn how you can proactively establish a line of communication and build trust with your colleagues. Next, you'll see the techniques you can use to create a strong connection that turns adversaries into allies. Finally, you'll get practical strategies for diverting adversarial conflict and constructively developing a solution, through communicating, connecting, and contributing.

4

ESTABLISH A LINE OF COMMUNICATION

THERE ARE THREE minutes left in your weekly team meeting and your teammates are packing up their stuff. Your leader asks everyone to quiet down so he can cover one last item. He informs you that the company is putting on a bake sale to raise money for a local hospital. *Really?* you think. *Like I need one more thing on my plate.* He doesn't give you many details, he simply tells you that he got an email from his boss, that all departments are pitching in, and that he needs volunteers. You paste on a smile and sign up to be a baker.

Racking your brain for what to make, you settle on your favorite carrot muffin recipe, the one that wins raves from your friends every time. The morning of the sale, you walk into the cafeteria with your tray of scrumptious, golden, crispy-topped muffins, feeling proud of your homemade contribution while giving John side-eye for bringing the box of store-bought powdered donuts. Your boss takes one look at your muffins, scrunches up his face in disgust, and says, "Muffins aren't fun! Who's going to buy carrot muffins at a bake sale?!" Are you actually being publicly chastised for baking the wrong thing for a bake sale? You respond feebly, "But you never said that it needed to be fun; you just said to bake for the bake sale." Your boss walks over to the vending machine, returns with a pack of M&M's, and says, "I'll fix it!" as he starts poking candy into your beautiful muffins. What a waste.

I know the bake sale is a silly example, but it's representative of a pattern I see all too frequently in organizations. Your manager hastily communicates sketchy instructions, which you follow to the best of your ability. Then you learn, after the fact, that your work wasn't what the boss was looking for. You are forced to retrofit or even discard your first draft, making your initial efforts utterly futile. What's most frustrating about the bake sale conflict, like so many others, is that it was completely predictable and avoidable.

Engage Early

When you don't establish an effective line of communication with your boss up front, trust disappears, and you set yourself up for conflict later. You can eliminate the majority of conflicts by investing in proactive, clear, and transparent discussion that bolsters trust from the start. Effective communication is a key part of the conflict code. Your efforts will be rewarded with greater alignment and more confidence. Think about how you can establish strong dialogue with your manager, your teammates, your direct reports, and your colleagues across the organization. A little time invested in getting on the same page with these stakeholders up front will avert significant conflicts later.

Communicating with Your Boss

The most obvious person with whom you need to establish a line of communication is your manager. Having open and candid discussions with your boss will significantly reduce the amount of conflict you need to endure and will make any unavoidable conflicts much less unpleasant. I know some people are nervous to ask their managers too many questions, but remember it's your boss's job to set you up to be successful, so don't be sheepish about asking for the guidance you need to be effective.

The first and simplest way to inoculate yourself against conflict with your manager is to get clear on what he wants before you start any assignment. Unfortunately, not enough people stop and clarify expectations before diving into the work. Does that sound like you? Do you accept vague directions and struggle along hoping you're on the right track? Perhaps it's because you want to demonstrate a can-do attitude. Or maybe you think it's embarrassing to admit that you didn't understand the initial instructions. I'll tell you what's really embarrassing: pretending everything is fine and then delivering an inferior product. Your boss won't know whether to doubt your listening skills, your motivation, or your competence. You can avoid that unnecessary conflict by addressing potential areas of misalignment *before* you start the work.

In the bake sale example, the entire conflict could have been averted by asking the following questions: "What kind of bake sale is this? What types of items would be appropriate?" That would have tipped you off to your boss's desire to have, in his words, "fun" treats. Then, after choosing your recipe, you could have checked back in to make sure you were on track before you invested any time or resources. "I'm thinking carrot and zucchini muffins. They're so colorful and fun, how does that sound?" Sure, you probably still would have taken the ribbing from your boss for your veggie version of "fun," but at least you would have avoided the indignity of having M&M's shoved into your muffins.

Unfortunately, the frenetic pace in most organizations is probably causing your leader to shortchange planning. I see so many managers who think shortcutting planning will get them to the finish line more quickly. The irony is that rather than making things faster, shortchanging the instructions leads to more time in editing and rework and ultimately later delivery.

Reduced speed isn't the only nasty consequence of rushing the planning phase. Failing to clearly communicate expectations sets up an interpersonal conflict when the work is reviewed. Learning after the fact that your work wasn't on target erodes trust and zaps morale. Your boss is angry with you for not delivering, and you are angry with your boss for not being clear.

The alternative to setting up a conflict debt at the outset of a project is to establish the line of communication right at the start. If you don't have a clear picture of what is expected of you, don't proceed. Instead, ask questions to fill in the context, understand the request, and clarify what good work would look like. For example, you could ask, "Where did this project come from?" "What are they looking for?" "What are the most important parts of this?" and "What are you looking for in the finished product?" Then once you've started your work, check in to confirm that you're on the right track. You will save yourself considerable time, effort, and anguish if you share your recipe and let your boss taste the batter before anything is fully baked.

Communicating with Your Teammates

With your teammates, the power dynamic isn't as clear as it is with your boss, making it easier to leave your expectations unspoken—great kindling for conflict. I get that you don't want to seem like Mr. or Ms. Bossy Pants, but I'm not suggesting you start bossing your teammates around. The point is to make sure you're all on the same page about who is doing what and how your work intersects.

Mistrust can creep in very quickly when roles and responsibilities aren't clear. When you have overlapping responsibilities, the risk is that you feel like your teammates are meddling, whereas when there are gaps in accountabilities, you can find people appointing blame when a ball is dropped. Don't let your team walk headfirst into these problems; instead, go through each aspect of your assignments and make sure everyone is clear on who is on point for what. Where shared accountability is unavoidable, discuss the unique value each person will bring to the task.

With your teammates, it's important to not only share expectations but also to manage them. As workloads get higher and higher, it can be impossible to deliver everything on time and with the quality you'd like. It's important to negotiate workload issues with your teammates so you don't wind up letting them down. Use questions like, "I'm swamped, and I know you're waiting for my help on this presentation. If I could give you an hour today, what's the most important thing you need from me?" If you feel like you're going to miss a commitment, give your teammates enough warning that they can find another solution. Try saying, "I don't think I'm going to be able to get you that spreadsheet by Friday. Can we find another solution, so you aren't left waiting?" Both of these examples require you to have a mildly uncomfortable conversation early to head off a really unpleasant conflict later.

Communication across Teams

Getting aligned and heading off conflict with your boss and your team is relatively easy. That's because as members of the same team, you're ultimately working toward the same goals. You likely also have frequent opportunities to interact and build trust with people who are on your team. It's much more challenging when you have to work with people on other teams because you don't have existing relationships or obvious opportunities to build them. In a five-year study of 5,000 workers, management theorist Morten Hansen found that 46% of people feel there is a lack of trust in their collaborations across their organizations.[11] Without trust, it is much harder to establish shared goals and expectations and much more difficult to have a fruitful collaboration. People perceived as being very good at fostering trust performed much better than those who were not seen as trust builders. Wherever possible, establish a line of communication *before* you need it. Don't make the mistake of waiting until you need someone's help.

I know, it's a big ask. With the volume of work you're handling, it's understandable that you keep your head down until you need someone in another department to help you get your job done. Now imagine the consequences of waiting to connect until you need something urgently. You have little time to build rapport or demonstrate your good intentions, you just dive into the task at hand. "Hi, I'm Bob, I need a report on the traffic to the new site." This request

≡ ESTABLISH A LINE OF ≡

COMMUNICATION

BEFORE YOU NEED IT:

"DON'T WAIT

UNTIL YOU'RE

► THIRSTY ◄

TO DIG A WELL."

has come out of nowhere for your colleague: "Um, which department did you say you were from?" You burst on the scene asking for what you need but with little interest in his workload or priorities. You've probably triggered his "self-serving jerk" warning bells. You only increase that friction when you add, "Hey, this is *super* urgent, can I have it today?" If you wait until you need something to make contact, you are setting yourself up for conflict. Make an effort to establish a line of communication *before* you need it. As the old saying goes, "Don't wait until you're thirsty to dig a well."

Building Trust

Whether it's your boss, your teammates, or your colleagues across the organization, it's important to build trust proactively. If you have someone's trust, they will interpret your behavior more favorably and you'll find that you get the benefit of the doubt in sticky situations. Working through an uncomfortable situation with someone who trusts you will feel less confrontational and is less likely to turn into a conflict.

Trust isn't built in an instant, so you're wise to invest in proactively building trust with the people you work with. You can establish your trustworthiness at four different levels. First, you can create a *connection* so that your colleagues know you as a person and give you the room to be authentic. Second, you can earn *credibility*, so they will give you autonomy to get your work done instead of questioning you at every turn. Third, you can demonstrate your *reliability*, so you don't get micromanaged. Finally, you can ooze *integrity*, so people will be candid and vulnerable around you rather than being defensive and resistant. Each of these levels of trust can be established over time if you dedicate energy to it.

1. Create a Connection

At the most basic level, trust is about predictability. People who know you well will barely notice your behavior; even your weird idiosyncrasies will seem routine because they see them all the time. When you interact with someone you don't know as well, they are more likely to notice your behavior and more likely to interpret those idiosyncrasies as threatening. That's because people's brains are wired to notice things that are different and novel, particularly those that might pose a threat to them. Unless you form a connection with your colleagues, they are likely to see you as part of the out-group and someone to protect themselves against.

I once had thirty minutes to manufacture this connection with a group of executives. I was helping with the merger of two large insurance companies. While planning for the first session of the combined executive team, one of the leaders told me that his definition of success would be to "get rid of the *us* and *them*." As a psychologist, I had to tell him that there was no way to avoid in-groups and out-groups because humans form them naturally. I told him that what I could do was help everyone see that there are many ways to think of us and them.

At the start of the session, I positioned two flip charts, one in each corner of the room. On each was a sheet of paper with a label. One flip chart was labeled with the name of one legacy company; the second flip chart had the name of the other. I asked everyone to go stand beside the name of their former company. I did a little spiel about the power of us and them: "This is your tribe... yada, yada." Next, I had them peel off the label to reveal a second label beneath. One said, "Business Line Leader" and the other said, "Corporate Function Leader." Again, I asked them to stand beside the label that described their in-group. Now half of the leaders from each group shifted to the other board. The heads of finance, human resources, and marketing from both companies stood together staring down the heads of underwriting and claims. Although the legacy company was a powerful in-group, we quickly learned that so, too, was the functional versus business line categorization. "You guys are just the overhead," quipped one of the cocky business line leaders. "Good one," said his new colleague from the other company as they fist bumped. Success! We had formed a new cross-company in-group. We continued through a series of labels, some serious and business-related (accountant versus non-accountant) and some play-ful (prefer baked potato or fries). By the end of the exercise, each person had been in an in-group with every other person in the room. Suddenly, everyone had stronger connections.

You don't have to do an exercise like this to break down silos in your organization. Just make time to get to know the people with whom you might have to collaborate. Start with small gestures, such as sitting down beside someone you don't know at a meeting and introducing yourself. Then take a few seconds as you're packing up and walking out to get to know the person. You could say, "Our paths haven't crossed before; how long have you been in engineering?" Slowly, find opportunities to deepen the relationship by sharing information and asking questions. As soon as it feels appropriate, solicit help on something. "I'm working on a design for a new prod-uct and I'd love to get a perspective from outside my group. Can I send it to you?" Once the person has helped you, they'll immediately feel more connected. The goal is to give your colleague a sense of you as a person and as a teammate. You want to be a known quantity so that you're included in the in-group rather than being relegated to the nameless, faceless out-group. You want to be an us, not a them.

2. Earn Credibility

Once you create a connection, the next step in building trust is to establish your credibility. Without it, your manager, your teammates, and your colleagues won't have confidence that you can deliver. I bet you can relate to how anxiety-provoking it is to have to depend on someone you don't know to accomplish your goals. If your col-leagues are counting on you but they don't trust your abilities, you'll see a wide variety of dysfunctional behaviors. You could be on the receiving end of anything from a cuckoo colleague who hovers over you to one who sits back and distances themselves from the final product. The former leads to aggressive conflict and the latter to the passive-aggressive variety, neither of which is good for you. The antidote to letting concern about your competence create conflict is to build your credibility proactively.

You're probably thinking, *How do I earn credibility before I actually do something? Isn't credibility about my track record?* Yes, and . . . there are still a couple of ways to make people believe you're competent even before you deliver the goods. First, you can start by sharing your thinking about relevant issues. "I went to a conference last week and got some new ideas about how we could better manage our project. I'd love to grab a coffee and fill you in." You haven't actually *done* anything, but you've already got a leg up by showing that you're investing in your skills. If your colleague likes what you have to say, you'll continue to earn their confidence.

You won't necessarily get it right the first time. If your colleague doesn't like your ideas, a second way to build their confidence in you is to ask for their input. I know that sounds backward, but we humans are a bit strange. We think more highly of people when we think they like us. So, show your colleague that you value their perspective. "I'd love to hear how you would approach this." Just by being heard out, the person will increase their confidence in you. Investing to earn credibility with your colleagues is extremely important if you want to build trust, earn the benefit of the doubt, and avoid unnecessary conflict.

3. Demonstrate Reliability

As you move beyond the basic building blocks of connection and credibility, you can strengthen your colleague's trust in you by demonstrating your reliability. Even if you are the most competent person in the world, trust will disappear in an instant if you fail to meet your colleagues' expectations. I'll assume that you wouldn't drop the ball intentionally, but if you deliver something later than, less than, or even different from what your colleague expected, you will be branded as unreliable. Similar to how your colleagues react when they lack confidence in your capability, if they fear that you're unreliable, it could lead to anxious oversight and tiresome meddling.

To demonstrate reliability, verify that you have a shared view of each other's expectations. To bolster perceptions of your reliability even before you start to work, take a little extra time to be explicit about what you will do and by when. "My role on the team is to find sponsors for the conference. You're counting on me to have three sponsors worth $50,000 by the end of May. Is that right?" Then don't wait until the deadline to communicate. Remember this is less about *being* reliable and more about *being perceived* as reliable. Keep your colleagues' trust by sharing updates and milestones proactively. "It's only week two and I've got the first sponsor on board. They came in with $25,000, so we're on the right track." That will help your teammates rest assured that you are going to deliver.

Counterintuitively, if you want to be seen as reliable, you should also share your mistakes and failings, not just your successes. That will bolster confidence by making your colleagues feel like they are getting the straight goods. If you're in jeopardy of not delivering, *don't* hide it and hope you'll figure it out. Instead, give your team-mates a heads-up that there's an issue and involve them in your choice of a solution. The least reliable people are the ones who hide their struggles and leave no room for their colleagues to plan for con-tingencies. Demonstrating reliability requires open communication, even when it is uncomfortable.

4. Ooze Integrity

Finally, the most profound level is trust in your integrity. When your colleagues can be sure that you will act honestly, transparently, and in your shared best interest, then you will have cemented their trust in you. I know you know how important integrity is, but are you paying enough attention to how your colleagues perceive you—even in the moments where you're stretched to the limit? It's so easy to ruin your reputation for integrity in the difficult moments. Each time you apportion blame or shirk responsibility, you go down a notch in your colleagues' eyes. If you say one thing but do another, trust in you evaporates. If you feign support or even keep quiet when you're together and then complain or criticize when your colleague is out of earshot, you will do damage to your reputation in ways that will be difficult to repair. You want your colleagues to see you as a person of high integrity.

It's easier to think of ways to destroy your integrity rather than ways to proactively enhance it, but there are some secrets to being perceived as a person of good character. First, be open and candid, especially when there's something uncomfortable to say. You want your colleagues to know they can count on you to tell them the things that they need to hear. "I want you to hear this from me. Gary is concerned that you haven't included enough research in your report. He plans to raise it in the meeting this afternoon." Second, be vulnerable and transparent about your own struggles and concerns. "I'm working on this plan, but I'm worried that I don't have enough experience with supply chain. Do you have any suggestions on how I could pull in that perspective?" Finally, be quick to admit mistakes. "I got really defensive in that meeting and that showed badly on our project. I'm really sorry. Here's what I'm going to do to fix it." It's better to stay on the high road and to ooze integrity by having the courage to have the hard conversations. If you find yourself on the low road, do everything in your power to reestablish your colleagues' trust.

All of these trust issues come back to the same basic idea: your boss, your teammates, and your colleagues from across the organization all depend on you for their success. That dependence can make them nervous, and turn a team project into a powder keg. Keep the situation calm by establishing trust before the moment of truth. Get to know your colleagues and make them feel like you're fighting on the same side. Earn their confidence by proving your credibility even before it's tested. Demonstrate your reliability by aligning your expectations and making good on small promises so they know you'll come through on the big ones. At every turn, take the high road and find opportunities to show that you're a person of integrity. All of the investment in building trust *up front* will pay off in less conflict, or at least more productive conflict. Those who trust you will give you the benefit of the doubt.

Increasing Your Trust in Others

Thus far, I've focused on how *you* can become trustworthy in the eyes of your colleagues. You also need to consider the opposite direction: how can you increase your trust in them? You might think that sounds strange... "Doesn't my colleagues' behavior determine whether or not they are trustworthy?" Well, partly, but you have a lot more control over it than you think. Trust is not objective. It can't be measured like the temperature. It's inside your head. You choose whether you trust or mistrust someone.

Don't believe me? Do the thought experiment for yourself and you'll see that trust isn't objectively tied to behavior. For instance, imagine a person whom you trust implicitly. Now imagine they do something that has a negative impact on you. Chances are you rationalize this as situational and find ways to continue trusting the person: "She didn't mean to cause problems for me. This project was just set up badly from the beginning." In the opposite case, someone you don't trust can do something very helpful and supportive for you and you'll probably find a rationale to continue mistrusting them: "Oh sure, that's what he did *this* time. I'm sure it was only because it was convenient for him." Research has shown exactly this pattern. For people in our out-group (whom we're unlikely to trust), we attribute negative behavior to the person's *character*, whereas for members of our in-group, we attribute negative behavior to the *situation*. That error in judgment, referred to as the "ultimate attribution error," just reinforces what we already believe about someone.[12]

This vicious cycle is why it's so difficult to restore your trust once it has been damaged. That's because once someone has abused your trust, you feel vulnerable. You naturally try to protect yourself, but your defensive positioning triggers a self-protective reaction in the other person and things spiral downward. Instead of protecting and defending, your option is to start giving trust, even if it hasn't been earned. This strategy is what I call a "trust hack." It makes use of a surprising bit of psychology. We all know that how we feel about something affects what we do about it (attitude leads to behavior). Fewer people know that the reverse is also true: we often infer how we feel about something by how we behave (behavior leads to emotion). You can use this hack to your advantage when restoring trust.

Think of one situation where you don't trust a colleague and they don't trust you. Now ask yourself what you would do in that situation if you *did* trust that person. Then take one small but meaningful action in that direction. Make sure to be explicit about what you're doing so the other person recognizes it. For example, you might not trust someone to advocate on your behalf in a cross-functional meeting. If you did trust them, maybe you would skip the meeting and use the extra hour to get some work done. Don't wait to feel it, just do it. Try saying the following, "If you're attending that meeting, I'm comfortable that you'll represent me. Here are the three points that I think need to be covered." Act like you trust the person, even if you don't.

Acting as if you trust someone will set off two virtuous cycles. First, behaving as if you trust the person will create cognitive dissonance in you (because of the gap between how you feel and what you're doing). If you stick with the trusting behavior, the only way to reduce the dissonance will be to change how you feel about the person: *I am letting him represent me in this meeting, so therefore I must trust him*. That will improve the experience of the relationship from your side.[13] Second, seeing evidence that you trust him will start to change how your colleague thinks about you (as I mentioned before, we like people who like us). Your colleague will perceive your increased trust, which will improve the experience of the relationship from his side. When both of you experience the relationship differently, it is already improved. Those improvements in perception will lead to more trusting behavior and the downward spiral will reverse direction.

If the trust in your relationship has really been damaged, you'll probably need to stick with this plan for a while before your colleague gets past the "too good to be true" phase. But keep going. Unless your colleague has a personality disorder, he will feel the responsibility that comes with your trust and behave accordingly. I realize that this approach has risks. It *is* possible that the person will abuse your trust. But think of it as a game of odds: if you do nothing to repair the trust, you can be fairly certain that things will deteriorate; if you take a risk and trust first, there is a chance that things will get better. And that's a chance worth taking.

If you want to improve trust, start with a positive assumption. When you do, your words will change, your tone will change, and your body language will change. In response to the openness in your position and tone, the other person will respond in kind. Then the cycle will become virtuous, not vicious. It's hard to believe it until you try it, but acting as though you trust someone will change how they behave and ultimately justify your trust in them.

The secret to reducing the frequency and severity of unhealthy conflict is to engage with key stakeholders before there is an issue that needs to be addressed. Establishing a line of communication and building trust before the moment of truth is the first step in the conflict code. When things occasionally go poorly in a relationship where you trust one another, you'll both be more likely to blame the problems on the situation, which leaves you as allies trying to solve a problem, rather than as adversaries battling against one another. Establishing communication early inoculates you from conflict.

In Brief

- Conflicts often arise because we act without a clear understanding of what's expected of us.

- It's important to establish a line of communication and to build trust (with your boss, your teammates, and your colleagues in other departments) before there is an issue to address.

- To build trust, create a connection that allows your colleagues to understand you as a person. The more predictable they find your behavior, the more they will trust you.

- Earn credibility even before you have a track record by asking good questions and demonstrating how you will tackle your work.

- Demonstrate reliability and show your colleagues that you will prioritize their needs.

- Ooze integrity by being transparent, especially if you are struggling.

- Actively strengthen your trust in your colleagues by behaving as though you trust them, even before you do.

CREATE A CONNECTION

JOE IS THE vice president of underwriting at a mid-sized insurance company. Several months ago, Joe had to fill a key position on his team, the head of the project management office (PMO). Although he was tempted to look externally, he received an application from Sue, a longtime employee who had always been a strong project manager. Joe's boss, Charlie, was a big fan of Sue and wanted Joe to give her the chance. Joe had some reservations about her ability to manage such a big portfolio, but overall he thought she was a good fit and gave her the job.

A few months into her new role, Sue was struggling. She was getting too deep in the weeds micromanaging her replacement and couldn't cope with those tasks in addition to all of her new responsibilities. Joe was frustrated that the PMO hadn't made the kind of gains he was hoping for, but he was trying to cut Sue some slack and give her time to learn her new role. That was until Sue dropped the ball on a very important automated billing project. Under Sue's watch, two project streams missed their deadlines, incurring significant financial penalties from the technology vendor. Rather than take ownership of the miss, Sue blamed everyone else for the delays. The last straw was when she started yelling at Joe in his team meeting.

She accused Joe of not supporting her, blamed him for overloading her, and then stormed out.

Joe is ready to let Sue go. Now Charlie, the chief operating officer and Joe's boss, is involved. He's trying to talk Joe into giving Sue another chance. Charlie suggests that they could change Sue's role to take off some of the pressure. If they assigned some of the other projects in the portfolio to the senior project coordinators, she could focus on the automation project. Alternatively, they could rely more heavily on the consulting firm to take on some of the project management. Charlie is determined to make it work.

No matter what Charlie suggests, Joe isn't biting. "Nope, that won't work" is his response to every suggestion. Charlie is at a loss for what to do next. He doesn't want to force Joe to keep Sue, but he feels like it might be coming to that. Joe feels like everyone involved is framing him as the bad guy. He suspects that Charlie intends to force him to keep Sue, but why doesn't he just come right out and say so? Joe doesn't understand how Charlie could possibly want to keep Sue at the company after she screwed up so badly.

Allies, Not Adversaries

The situation with Joe and Charlie has devolved into an ugly conflict. You might expect Joe and Charlie, as two leaders, to have been on the same side in this fight, but somehow they have become adversaries. Emotions are running high and there is little effort on either man's part to understand where the other is coming from. The animosity between them is clear. Joe doesn't like Charlie's proposed solutions and is frustrated that he's not being given the autonomy to make the call about Sue. Charlie is irritated by Joe's unwillingness to negotiate changes to Sue's role that would help her succeed. How did they get on opposite sides of this issue?

The answer, of course, is that they got on opposite sides by failing to listen and by becoming completely disconnected from one another. Actually, the problem started even before they stopped listening to one another. The reason they got into this situation in the first place is because they aren't saying what they need to in order to express their own frustrations. They haven't done a good job articulating what's important to them. Nothing that has yet been said out loud has unveiled the true source of the argument or helped to explain why it has become so heated. Without that information, they can't get what they need to stop fighting and start problem-solving. That's when they call me.

I sit down to talk with the two of them. I start by asking Joe, "Charlie is giving you several options for how you could modify Sue's job description to make it more manageable in the future. What do you think about those options?"

Joe's giant sigh tells me he is exasperated by how hard it is to get Charlie to understand his perspective, but he's trying to stay calm when he responds, "I'm not sure. I don't know if that will help. I'm worried that Sue is happier in the detail of a single project and that she's in over her head when she has to manage multiple projects. If we let her stay on, what's going to stop *this* from happening again?" Joe waves his hands wildly as he says "this," giving me something to pick up on.

"What is 'this' that you're referring to?"

"Sue dropping the ball, getting our projects behind, yelling and screaming and blaming me for all the problems." Joe's voice cracks as he speaks. Now we are getting somewhere. He is giving us the clues about the real source of the problem.

"Sounds like you're still thinking about Sue's last day in the office, the meeting where she attributed the problems in the PMO to you, is that right?"

Leaning into the emotions created the candor I was looking for. Joe responds, "Of course I'm thinking about that meeting! She humiliated me in front of my entire team. I was completely blindsided! And now you want to just let her march back in here, asking the people who she threw under the bus to pick up her slack. That's a big ask, given that she hasn't apologized to me or any of the people she blamed for her mistakes. I just don't get it!"

There it was. This wasn't a fight about job duties. Charlie was never going to solve the issue by changing Sue's responsibilities. This was a fight about how Sue made Joe feel. He was caught off guard and embarrassed in front of his team. Sue accused him of being an uncaring leader, which was completely contrary to how he thought of himself. She had caused a lot of pain for him and for the rest of the team and she had never said, "Sorry." Joe wasn't worried about whether they could change Sue's *job*, he was worried about whether they could change her *character*.

I reflected back what I heard, as much for Charlie's benefit as for Joe's. "For you, this is about Sue's accountability and ownership. She didn't take ownership of the workload in the first place and she still hasn't taken accountability for her behavior in the meeting. Is that a fair assessment? You're worried that if you bring her back into the role, she still won't take accountability and your whole team will be at risk." I simply verbalize what Joe had been feeling but not communicating, all along.

Turns out Joe is a stickler for accountability. He's patient and generous with employees who admit that they are struggling, but otherwise he assumes that no news is good news. He has no time for people who don't take ownership of their challenges and a strong distaste for someone who would blame her problems on others. Sue had violated Joe's core value of accountability. To make matters worse, Sue's accusations that Joe hadn't lived up to his own accountabilities as a leader had shaken his self-confidence. It was going to be a tough road back.

Now we have half of the issue on the table. Solving this problem will require an apology from Sue and some assurance that she will take greater accountability in the future. What about Charlie? Why is a senior leader defending someone who had cost the firm tens of thousands of dollars in penalties? Now it's Joe's turn to listen and learn.

"Charlie," I say, "now that you know how raw this is for Joe, you can understand why it's hard for him to stay open to the idea of keeping Sue on. Can you help him understand what's at stake for you in this situation?" I try to make it clear to both men that the right to be heard comes with the responsibility to listen.

"I think we owe it to Sue to try to make this work," Charlie says. "It was an important decision when we promoted someone from within the company and it would look bad if she didn't succeed. It might cause other people to think twice before applying for promotions and that would have a terrible impact on morale."

It doesn't quite add up. Surely people would understand if someone who made a major error was penalized. I still wasn't clear what was at the heart of the issue for Charlie. Time for more questions. "Tell me more about the impact of letting somebody who was promoted from within struggle."

Charlie doesn't really have a response. He fumbles around and finally tells us what he was really thinking: "To be fair, I just don't know. I think this whole thing might be my fault."

Ah, guilt. Guilt is a powerful emotion that's tied to deep beliefs. When I see signs that someone is feeling guilty about their behavior, I know I'm headed in the right direction. He only needs a little prompt to keep going: "Say more..."

"I wasn't paying enough attention." Charlie stops talking to me and looks directly at Joe. "Sometimes you can have very high standards," he continues. "I'm not sure you make room for people to admit when they're overloaded. You have such a high capacity and I think your people are afraid of letting you down. I've known Sue for ten years, I should have known she would try to play the hero. I feel like maybe I set this up for failure from the beginning. I would feel terrible about firing Sue without giving her another chance."

Charlie has a strong sense of loyalty to his people. He feels a powerful obligation as their leader, one which he fears he has fallen down on in this case. Sure, he wants to give Sue another chance, but really, he wants to give himself another chance.

What had started as a negotiation about job duties has morphed into a profound dialogue about character, accountability, and leadership—values. Now it is clear that a solution will need to solve for greater transparency and responsibility from Sue, more realistic expectations from Joe, and more supportive oversight from Charlie. The hard work is done. We know what a good solution will look like, and now we just need to hammer out the details.

The moment the two men connect with one another, the tenor of the conversation changes dramatically. Charlie feels the weight of Joe's embarrassment and self-doubt and he is careful to consider the impact on Joe when he lists the options. Up to this point, he's been so focused on Sue's feelings that he missed Joe's point of view altogether. Similarly, Joe has now seen Charlie take accountability for his role in the fiasco, which makes him feel less singled out. They are back to being allies trying to solve a problem rather than adversaries locked in a battle.

As Joe and Charlie's story illustrates, to get the issues on the table so that you can start problem-solving, you need to work through three layers of information: the facts, the feelings, and the values.

Facts Don't Solve Fights

It's easy to be misled into thinking that opposing facts and information are the cause of conflicts you face at work; they seldom are. When all that's in question in a dispute is the validity or relative importance of different information, you'll experience it as solving a problem, not having a fight. As soon as the source of the issue is something buried beneath the facts in the realm of conflicting values and motives, that's when it will start to look, feel, or smell like a conflict. In that case, the facts are just a diversion your colleague creatively curates to justify how they feel and what they believe.

It's understandable if you're angry that your colleagues would try to bullshit you by sharing only the facts that support their case. But it's not actually you they are trying to deceive. Years of psychology research suggest that they are actually deceiving themselves—the first and most important audience for their elaborate rationalization. As humans, we want our behavior to make sense, so we concoct great stories about why we do what we do. We do and say what we believe and then try to make our actions and positions seem rational by assembling facts that justify them. Neuropsychologist Michael Gazzaniga describes it as trying to keep your story coherent.[14] You do what you feel or believe, *then* collect the facts to create a narrative that's consistent.

That's why the facts your colleagues share are not something solid you can grasp onto in an argument. If the first set of facts doesn't work to convince you of what they want, there will always be other facts to try out. Until you get past the facts to what the person really wants, you'll continue to face a barrage of mostly deceptive information. Mostly.

Insights from Information

The facts themselves might be deceptive, but they're valuable. They're the only clues you have to divine where the values and beliefs lie. Your first strategy should therefore be to gather as much information as possible from the facts you're given.

There are plenty of insights to be gleaned; you just need to sift through to find the good stuff. The first thing to notice is what information the person chooses to share. Equally important, what did they omit? What did they try to pass off as fact that was really opinion or judgment? What did they say and how did they say it? All of these answers provide clues about what matters to the person you're speaking with.

You can learn a lot from the facts people use to support their position. Pay attention to the aspects of the problem that they choose to focus on; for example, "You made three points of how this approach would benefit the marketing team. Do you see marketing as the primary beneficiary of this project?" More specifically, you can pick up on the types of facts they are emphasizing, such as, "You mentioned increased speed, better prioritization, and less rework. Is your plan an efficiency play from your perspective?"

The facts provide the entrée into a deeper conversation. You encounter the least resistance if you anchor your questioning to information the person has given you. In that way, you're signaling that you will start the discussion on their terms. There are many routes you can choose to deepen the connection. You can ask for more information: "Your take on improving prioritization of marketing projects is interesting. Tell me more about it." You can paraphrase what the person is saying to clarify the different issues: "I'm hearing you say we need a different way for product development to engage marketing *and* a different way of project managing once the initiatives are in place. Is there anything I'm missing?" To ensure you're really on the same wavelength, you can ask the person to define the terms they're using: "You used the word 'initiative.' What size of projects are you thinking would be eligible for this new process?"

While you're tuned in to the facts that your colleague *is* sharing, it's just as important to listen for what they *aren't* saying. If the person emphasizes one part of the issue while neglecting another, you learn about what's important to them (and what's not). If they focus on one stakeholder and exclude others, you get another clue. If all the benefits they cite are financial, you might infer that they care less about intangible issues such as customer experience or employee engagement. If all they talk about are the intangibles, you might question how much weight they put on the financial side of the equation. Once you've asked a few questions about what your colleague said, throw in a question or two about what they didn't. "You talked about product development and marketing, but I'm curious that you didn't mention sales. What's your take on sales' role in this?" People exclude parts of an issue for different reasons. They might not know about them, they might think they're less important, or they might intentionally be trying to move the discussion away from facts that work against their case. Digging into what they aren't saying will also help you understand where the problem lies.

Once you've collected all the facts and information and dug around for the things your colleague didn't mention, you can pay attention to the third and final category: the faux facts. As your colleague makes their case, it's likely you'll hear one or more statements that seem like facts at first but soon reveal themselves as hollow judgments or opinions. The ratio of judgments to facts often goes up as an argument gets more heated. Take note as your colleague makes unsubstantiated claims. In the marketing scenario, you might hear your colleague talk about the current process as "a slog," or about the "burden that product development puts on them." You might hear judgments on the positive side, too, such as the "advantage of the new approach," or the "relief" of systematizing the process. Most people have been socialized to avoid getting overly emotional at work. If you listen carefully, you'll see the emotions leak out in the judgments and opinions they try to pass off as facts.

Follow the Emotion

Once you've gathered all the information from the facts, your second strategy is to pay attention to the person's emotions. Rather than avoiding the emotion in the conversation, you want to move toward it because where the emotion lies is where the solution is buried. When you broach the emotional aspects of an issue, tie your comments to something you observed. Follow the formula of: 1) describing the behavior; 2) sharing your hypothesis; and 3) asking a question. An example is "You used the word 'critical' three times. I get the sense that you feel a real sense of urgency to move on this. What makes the timing so important?"

Because showing emotion is countercultural in so many organizations, you might only be picking up how your colleague feels from what they did, rather than from what they said. Just because your evidence is from body language rather than words doesn't mean the formula changes. You still need to describe what you saw, then ask a question to better understand. "As you were talking, your voice got quieter and quieter. Are you reticent to force the issue with product development?" Volume, pitch, eye contact, open or closed body position, leaning into or backing away from the table—each of these signals is worth investigating when you're trying to understand the root of a conflict.

As with facts and information, the emotion that is missing is just as important as what is there. If your colleague isn't excited about something they probably should be, there might be underlying concerns or anxiety. That's something worth investigating: "I expected you to be excited about marketing having greater control of the prioritization but from your tone of voice, it doesn't sound like it. Where are you at on this?" Keep in mind that someone who is exuding only positive vibes might be downplaying the risks of a proposed plan. Take notice of emotions that don't seem to match the situation. That's how you'll know that the proposed solution isn't solving for the things that really matter to them.

Going for Gold: Uncovering People's Values and Beliefs

Don't get too wrapped up in your colleague's emotions. Understanding their emotions is just a means to an end. You're their colleague, not their therapist. The reason you need to explore the emotions is because they lead the way to the third and most valuable strategy— uncovering the values and beliefs that are driving your colleague's behavior. In many cases, the person won't realize that their values are being violated. Without your help, they won't have access to what's bothering them or how to fix it. This is the point at which you can forge a strong connection and unearth the issues that need to be resolved to end the conflict and start solving the problem.

The formula for uncovering values and beliefs builds on the one for surfacing emotions. Again, you start with sharing what you are observing because their behavior is the most objective information you have. After describing what you see, add your perception of what they are feeling, then probe about what is beneath that emotion. For example, "When you were talking about the challenges with the production development process, you used the phrase 'putting on the brakes.' What do you see as the value of marketing in the product development process?" This open-ended question leaves lots of room for your colleague to reflect on what they value. Your search for solutions will go in different directions if the answer is "Marketing is here to weed out the crazy product ideas that no one would ever buy" versus "Marketing tries to push things through the process too quickly. We do a disservice to our products."

Listen to what your colleague puts in the plus and minus columns in the decision. What do they see as the upside and what risks or downsides are they focused on? If you want to unlock the conflict and create movement in a certain direction, you need to understand where your colleague is on both sides of the equation. To get a better sense of the levers on the plus side, you could ask, "What would make this worth doing for you?" To uncover their fears of the downside, ask, "What worries you about this approach?" As you listen and demonstrate your openness to the issues that matter most, you will uncover the critical aspects of the problem that you can work with as you problem-solve.

Taking the time to understand the facts, emotions, and values is to truly communicate. Communicate comes from the Latin for "make common." You only connect when the common understanding goes deeper than the intellectual arguments and into your colleague's values and motives. Unfortunately, you can't get there if you're doing all the talking.

When you get to a common understanding of your values, that's when you really become connected. That level of connection is worth the investment. Once you're really communicating with your colleagues, you'll be out of conflict mode and into problem-solving. That's the second step in the conflict code.

The Benefits of Getting to the Values

"Come on, Liane ... executives don't talk about emotions around the boardroom table!" asserted an incredulous VP of marketing at a multinational bank. We were in the midst of a very uncomfortable and intense team conversation about an issue that had been surfacing and resurfacing for months without being resolved. The argument was about their approach to managing a large regional office. This office had been part of an acquisition, and the company had allowed the office to run autonomously for three years since the merger. The leadership team was now fighting over when to integrate the office into their processes and systems. It seemed like a pretty standard business decision, but the fact that they hadn't resolved it in twelve months suggested that there was something more going on.

I was encouraging them to go beyond the intellectual arguments and to lean into the emotional issues if they wanted to resolve it. The conversations about system integration and workflows were masking the true source of the issue: a conflict between the leaders who valued operational excellence (who were driving for efficient and streamlined processes) and those who prioritized the strong culture (who wanted to protect the unique spirit in the regional office). By focusing the conversation on the nuts and bolts of integrating systems, they were ignoring what really mattered to one another. That decision was creating resistance and triggering divisive passive-aggressive behavior among the different factions on the team. We even had one team member lock herself in the bathroom, refusing to come out because she was so infuriated by her teammates' unwillingness to consider her point of view. Once I convinced everyone to be transparent about why they felt the way they did, the conversation became more productive.

They realized that the conflict they were having was being influenced by their biases, whether they admitted it or not. Making the emotional aspects explicit allowed everyone to discuss them and decide how they would weight those factors along with the facts in the case. Exposing the emotions increased their ability to control their impact on the ultimate decision.

The head of marketing had been worried about dragging emotions into the argument for fear it would slow them down and cause the conflict to drag on even longer. He kept telling everyone, "This is a business decision, it's not personal." He was surprised to realize that this reluctance to address the emotional subtext was what was causing them to revisit the issue without resolution. They were carrying

≡ COMMUNICATION ≡
IS, BY DEFINITION, NOT
· SOMETHING ·
YOU CAN ACCOMPLISH
ON YOUR OWN.
YOU CAN'T COMMUNICATE
TO SOMEONE,
YOU CAN ONLY COMMUNICATE
WITH THEM.

conflict debt. Acknowledging the conflicting values and beliefs that were the source of the emotions allowed everyone to relax, knowing that their concerns would be addressed in the solution. With that confidence, they were able to start problem-solving. Addressing the emotions helped them move through the conflict more quickly.

There was an even more important benefit of addressing the emotional aspects of this issue. When people's emotions were skewing their arguments, it was creating confusion and suspicion within the team. One team member, Kevin, had made comments that were particularly perplexing to his colleagues. He kept trying to argue that the company's processes were inefficient and that it was futile to impose them on the regional office. That got the head of operations in a bit of a tizzy. It was only after several questions that Kevin finally exposed his belief that the benefits of the strong culture far outweighed the potential gains of implementing common systems. Then everyone finally understood why he was complaining about the systems. In the meantime, he had engendered significant mistrust from the head of operations and the rest of the team. If Kevin's motives had been transparent from the beginning, the mistrust could have been avoided.

Treating emotions and values as two other data sets, alongside the factual data, allows you to work with all the components affecting your decision. That will help you understand all the factors that are contributing to the conflict. In contrast, trying to "keep the emotion out of it" will only drive the emotions underground where they will detract from effective decision-making and contribute to mistrust and dysfunction. Sticking to the facts might seem like the expedient route, but it will ultimately prolong the conflict.

Creating a Connection

Validation

There is a fourth and final strategy for creating a strong connection that will convert unproductive conflict into productive problem-solving: validation. Normally, our default reaction when we uncover a value that is at odds with our own is to invalidate how the person is reacting. If they express anxiety, your tendency is to say, "Don't worry. It will be fine." If they say the issue is about accountability, you say, "No, it's about pragmatism," and on and on.

In addition to questioning, contradicting, or trumping your colleague's comments, there are other ways you can destroy the connection you've worked hard to create. One way is to jump straight into your perspective without reference to what your colleague said. Another way is to become louder and more polarized with each volley—getting further apart rather than closer together. You can also resign yourself to more conflict by questioning your colleague's motives or challenging their relevance, competence, or preparation. But perhaps the most insidious way you can invalidate the person is by turning your eyes and your body away from the person you're arguing with and toward the other people present. There are so many ways you can signal that you aren't listening and that you don't care.

What a waste! You've gone to all the effort of listening and uncovering the feelings and values driving your colleague's behavior and then thrown it away with a response that signals that nothing they said landed with you. That will only infuriate them. Instead of overtly or covertly invalidating your colleague, find ways of conveying that, while you might not agree, you have heard and understood what they are saying.

I mentioned former FBI hostage negotiator Chris Voss in Chapter 2 and his story of likening compromise to leaving the house wearing one brown and one black shoe. Voss knows the value of validating firsthand. In *Never Split the Difference*, he describes the technique of "mirroring." To mirror the person, you use your speech pattern, body language, and words to show that you're in sync with them. In a hostage scenario, this means repeating back the last three words (or most important three words) that the hostage-taker said. It's a shortcut to creating a connection. And don't worry, people like to hear their words repeated so it doesn't feel manipulative.

Let's hope that not all the conflict in your organization feels like a hostage negotiation. For less hostile situations, there are many other approaches to validating. You need to choose one that feels right, so you can do it completely and authentically. When your validation isn't genuine, it will make the situation even more adversarial. Some of your options include commenting on the importance of the discussion: "I think this is a critical conversation that we need to hash out"; thanking them: "Thanks for raising this issue, I've been uncomfortable with where we're heading"; or paraphrasing their comments: "From your perspective, this is about accountability." Choose the one that's most authentic so it's clear you're being genuine, not manipulative.

Validating the other person is the fastest, most reliable way to short-circuit a conflict. It will reduce defensiveness, keep things issue-focused, and greatly increase the speed with which you get to a mutually agreeable solution. It's not as hard as it sounds because validating doesn't mean you agree with your colleague's point. It just sends the signal that you are invested in problem-solving as allies rather than arguing as adversaries.

Stronger Connections

So far, we've talked about four strategies for creating a strong connection: gleaning insights from information, exploring emotions, uncovering values, and validating what you find. In addition to these primary strategies, here are a few other tips that will help you forge a strong connection and convert a conflict into a problem-solving discussion.

Reduce the interference (physical or symbolic) between you and the other person. Come out from behind your desk and sit on the same side of any table. While you're at it, uncross your arms. Use the physical situation in a way that conveys that you want to work through the difficult situation as allies.

One caveat. There are times when the message you're delivering is too potent to deliver full bore. In those situations, creating a bit of distance can help the person you're in conflict with feel safer. In these cases, sit or stand beside the person and have the conversation while facing parallel to them. (This is an excellent technique for communicating with people who find looking each other straight in the eye too intense.)

If you don't have the benefit of being in the same location, you're at a distinct disadvantage when you try to form a connection. I have seen many conflicts go from a simmer to a boil because of the awkwardness of addressing issues remotely. Thankfully, we have so many tools available to improve the quality of the connection with remote coworkers. Use those snazzy video calls. They will ensure you have at least some of the body language cues that will help you find the source of the conflict.

Distance isn't just physical; it can also be intellectual. It's tempting when you're arguing with someone to try to outsmart them or talk circles around them. That might drive the conflict underground, but it certainly won't resolve it. **Strip out the jargon.** Cash in your $10 words for a few $2 ones. Choose language that clearly conveys the message without overshadowing it or obscuring it.

Here's another way you create distance: turn out the lights and try to win your argument with a snazzy PowerPoint presentation. I can assure you that deflecting everyone's gaze away from you and reading through a list of points will neither strengthen the connection nor reduce their resistance to you or your ideas. **Focus on two-way communication.** As I said, you need to communicate *with* people, not at them.

Once you've let go of those connection killers, you can start with a few good habits. **To reduce the intensity of conflict, talk in unofficial spaces.** Meeting rooms and offices create formality and distance. When you need to improve your connection with a colleague, find better settings. Try the cafeteria, a bench in the foyer, or take a walk and discuss a particularly difficult issue.

Finally, be vulnerable and take accountability. **Use the first-person active voice.** There's no faster way to sound like a pretentious clod than by using the passive voice, speaking in vague generalities, such as, "The presentation was rejected because of its brevity." Instead, take ownership: "I believed your presentation was too short, so I sent it back." The first-person active voice conveys ownership. It tells the other person that you're willing to be uncomfortable in service of honesty, transparency, and candor.

The good news is that you don't have to be perfect at any of this to forge a stronger connection. If you genuinely want to understand what is important to your colleague, even fumbling with awkward questions is fine. Admit when you're struggling. "I'm sorry, I really want to understand where you're coming from and I'm struggling to find the right questions." Even if you stop being curious and get defensive, admitting your mistake will only strengthen the bond: "I keep interjecting my needs. I apologize. Let's go back to what you're trying to accomplish." The right motives are more important than the perfect words.

Organizational conflicts drag on and get personal and uncomfortable when you keep trying to solve the wrong problem. Unfortunately, your colleague probably won't tell you the real problem because it's not rational or logical; it's just what they believe or what they want, and they've been taught that no one will give credence to feelings and values. The longer you ignore the true issues, the more frustrated your colleague will feel, the more heated the discussion will become, and the more entrenched each side will get. If you invest in creating a strong connection, and really trying to understand where your colleague is coming from, you'll find your adversary suddenly becomes your ally. It will cease to be a fight and become two people working together to solve a problem.

In Brief

- Making the effort to create a strong connection with a person will allow you to problem-solve as allies rather than fight as adversaries.

- When a discussion gets heated, the facts and information presented provide excellent clues about what is important to the players. Pay attention to what is (and isn't) said to zero in on what's at stake.

- Explore the feelings and emotions the person is signaling with their language and their body language. Where emotions are present, it's likely that there are more substantive issues you haven't yet exposed.

- Use questions and observations to uncover the values and beliefs that underlie their position. It's the values and beliefs that will unlock the solution to the conflict.

- Regardless of whether or not you agree with the person, validate what they are saying to ensure they feel heard and understood.

- Use everything at your disposal to strengthen the connection you have with the other person, including your physical situation, your language and tone, and your body language.

6

CONTRIBUTE TO
A SOLUTION

I AM FACILITATING THE leaders of a prominent performing arts organization through a team effectiveness process. Multiple times during the day, members of the team have referred to a "budget issue" as an example of what's not working. I've decided to dive into the issue in hopes it will provide an opportunity to get them working through conflict more effectively.

As they start to talk about the budget, I realize it isn't a pretty picture. A $2 million shortfall in funding means they will have to cut expenses and won't be able to produce some of the ambitious programs they had planned. The discussion is tense as they wrestle with what to do.

Mary Beth, the head of fundraising, chimes in. "I think we should release the budget to the board of directors showing the $2 million deficit." She sits back in her chair looking pleased with her proactive solution.

Howard, the finance leader, is not impressed. "Are you kidding? We have a fiduciary responsibility to balance the budget. I would be failing to do my job if I didn't send them a balanced budget!" His comment is dripping with condescension.

I can see Mary Beth deflating. She is determined to change their fate and frustrated with Howard for being resigned to the painful cuts. It is clear that Howard is not backing down on his balanced budget stance. They are already digging in their heels and getting ready for a fight.

Problems, Not Solutions

Mary Beth jumped straight to a solution without getting agreement on the problem, and that triggered a conflict. Unfortunately, many of us are taught to jump straight to solving the problem. I learned the "come with a solution" rule from the first manager I ever worked for. He was a sleek, silver-haired consultant who valued self-reliance and had zero time for drama. I was trained to think through my concerns and have a recommendation ready to share. That advice has served me well managing relationships with bosses. I learned that coming prepared with a solution makes you look proactive, insightful, and accountable.

The problem starts when you apply this same "come with a solution" approach to solving problems that you don't own. Proposing a solution to someone else's problem can be misinterpreted in many ways. Your colleague might think you're meddling where you don't belong, doubting their ability to address the issue, or trying to score brownie points with the boss. Suddenly the proactive, take-charge behavior that made you a hero to your boss can make a colleague think you're an obnoxious know-it-all. Worse, if your solution misses the mark, you might come off as clueless and have your credibility take a hit. That's exactly what happened to Mary Beth.

I recognize what happened and ask both Howard and Mary Beth to pause and rewind. Rather than attacking her idea, I ask Howard to be curious about it. Howard is willing to give it a try. "Mary Beth, what are you trying to achieve by showing the board the deficit?"

She's quick with a response. "I just don't think the board has enough urgency around fundraising. If they knew all of the amazing ideas that we're giving up, I think they'd write a bigger check or make a few more calls." Mary Beth is articulate and compelling.

Katarina, the artistic director, immediately jumps in. "I couldn't agree more! I think they just accept what we tell them we're doing and don't push hard enough to allow us to do more. I've always felt the board needs a greater sense of urgency!"

Katarina's perspective carries significant weight with everyone on the team. If she thinks Mary Beth is right about the board being complacent, it is strong support for her argument.

Conflict Strategies for Nice People

So where do we go from here? Mary Beth and Katarina want to increase the transparency about the financial situation to the board, and Howard wants to demonstrate that he's living up to his responsibilities as the financial steward of the organization. The team needs a way of working through the situation calmly. They need an approach that will get to the heart of the issue, expose the conflicting priorities, and still feel collaborative.

I'm going to give you six techniques you can use to contribute to a solution to a conflict—the third part of the conflict code. I call these six techniques the Conflict Strategies for Nice People. Each one is designed to broach the uncomfortable discussion in a way that's minimally aversive and unlocks a workable solution. The strategies work in different situations and for different reasons. What they all have in common is they make use of the listening and validation approaches I shared in Chapter 5. Make sure you're fluent in those fundamental techniques before moving on to the conflict strategies.

1. Two Truths

The budget example is the perfect opportunity to use a conflict strategy I call the Two Truths. To use the Two Truths technique, follow these steps. First, validate your colleague's perspective by repeating it. If possible, ask an open-ended question to understand what's beneath their position. Once you have reflected their view and confirmed that you've understood their perspective, write it down somewhere that you can both see it: "Truth #1: we need to increase the sense of urgency among board members." Now you can add your perspective. "For me, this is about demonstrating our good stewardship of the organization." To the extent possible, add some color about why this matters to you. Do some of the heavy lifting of uncovering your feelings and values for the person. "I take my job as the finance lead really seriously. I really love this organization and don't want to see us get into financial troubles like so many other arts organizations." Next, frame your perspective as a truth and write it alongside Truth #1. "Truth #2: we need to show a balanced budget." Now you and everyone else in the discussion is staring at two truths spelled out on the board. Your job is to solve the problem assuming both are true. It will feel less like conflict and more like doing algebra.

The Two Truths is a great technique to use when a colleague makes a statement or an assertion you disagree with. Your disagreement might be relatively innocuous, such as if you think the person is paying attention to the wrong part of the problem. Alternatively, it might be quite severe, like when Howard interpreted Mary Beth's suggestion as reckless.

Regardless of the severity of your disagreement, your typical reaction to someone recommending a solution you don't agree with is to contradict them or try to trump them with your own point of view. It reminds me of the 1980s commercials for Miller Lite beer where two sides always fight over whether Miller Lite "tastes great" or is "less filling." Unfortunately, your colleague's natural reaction to someone contradicting them is probably to push back a little harder. That only entrenches each side in their original position; it doesn't give you a chance to move forward.

Instead of creating a tug-of-war, where you're pulling in opposition to one another, the Two Truths gets you on the same side to solve two separate but related problems. The fundamental premise of the Two Truths is that the other person doesn't have to be wrong for you to be right. It's possible for both of your perspectives to be true.

In the arts organization, the solution comes easily once they can see the two truths. The answer takes about five seconds: they prepare one page showing all the line items of the budget, including the ones they have to cut. They draw a line to delineate the funded and unfunded items, making it clear that one of the performances that the board was excited about is still without funding. The budget adds up, but the gap between their ambitions and their means is now clear. What started as a nasty conflict between "You don't know what it means to be an executive" and "You don't care about this organization" was resolved with everyone feeling good about their group approach.

The Two Truths technique short-circuits conflict by signaling to your colleague that you are prepared to listen to and accept their version of the situation. When you are willing to entertain their perspective, your colleague feels encouraged to reciprocate by opening up to yours. As both of you grapple with finding a solution that solves both problems, you shift into problem-solving mode, which is inherently collaborative instead of combative.

2. Root Cause

Two Truths should be your default approach when you disagree with someone's assessment of the problem. Sometimes, you don't disagree about the problem; you only take issue with your colleague's proposed solution. In that case, you can use the Root Cause strategy. Root Cause is a useful approach when you get the sense that you might be aligned on the problem, but you're still miles apart on the solution.

As I discussed in the Problems, Not Solutions section, it can cause friction when someone proposes a plan that oversteps their authority. If your colleague does this to you, you might feel offended that they didn't trust you to solve the problem. Your defensiveness causes you to ignore the fact that you're aligned about the problem, and it sends you straight into battle over the proposed solution. That's not going to foster a healthy discussion. Instead of becoming distracted by an untenable solution, stay focused on the problem. By agreeing that there is an important issue to be resolved, even if you don't agree with your colleague's initial proposal, you'll position yourself on the same side and create openness to exploring potential solutions.

I was working with a team that was struggling to deal with higher than normal turnover. They were trying to figure out what to do about it when one of the team members, Jess, proposed using a retention bonus for the top 25% of employees. It's an understatement to say that this idea didn't go down too well. Rose, the HR advisor, was taken aback by that suggestion. She knew what that would cost and how it would throw their budget out of whack. Rose wasn't the only one. Multiple people fired back at Jess with all the reasons why a retention bonus wasn't a good idea: "What if the top 25% all up and leave after we pay out? Won't that set a precedent and leave us having to pay for people's loyalty from now on?" I didn't hear anyone disagreeing with Jess that the turnover was a problem, so I suggested it was a great spot to use the Root Cause strategy.

I modeled it for them. "Jess, you think we have too much turnover and you'd like to implement retention bonuses." She nodded. Good, on to the next step. "What led you to suggest retention bonuses?" Jess thought about my question for a second and then responded, "We've had four people in the last three months talk about compensation in their exit interviews." Jess had heard compensation mentioned and locked onto it as the cause of the problem. I encouraged her to think about other potential causes: "Some people are mentioning compensation as their reason for leaving. What are some of the other reasons they're citing for quitting?" Jess deferred to Rose, the HR representative who conducted the exit interviews. Rose shed a little more light on the issue: "In my experience, it's easy for people to complain about compensation, but from my discussions with these folks, the bigger issue was that they didn't feel like we value them."

Rose was in complete agreement with Jess that something needed to be done about turnover, but she knew they couldn't jump to money as the only answer. "Retention bonuses might be one part of the solution," Rose said. "I'm also wondering if we need to do other things to show our top employees how much we value them." Once they found common ground, Rose trialed a resolution: "What if we gave retention bonuses to our top five people and did a round of individual development planning with everyone? Then we can revisit the merit increases and adjust their compensation for the start of the new year."

Using the Root Cause technique focuses on the fact that your colleague has raised a good idea, rather than on the fact that they proposed a poor solution. From that starting point, you will find more openness to explore different avenues to solve the problem while also minding any constraints. When you agree with the assessment of the problem but disagree with the solution, the Root Cause technique will help you find a path forward.

3. Question the Impact

The Two Truths or Root Cause strategies work when you're willing to believe that your colleague's perspective is true, or at least has some merit. There will be situations where you can't in all good conscience (or in the presence of evidence to the contrary) agree with your colleague's version of the truth. In those cases, don't use the Two Truths or Root Cause strategies because you won't be able to use them genuinely. The good news is that you have other options, one of which is the Impact technique.

The Impact technique is a great approach when someone proposes a bad idea that you know will wreak havoc (on your team, your customers, or your business). It's also useful when you don't know enough about the proposed solution to assess if it's a good idea or not. I had to use the Impact technique while working in my job at the HR consulting firm. Our firm was organized into regions with the business being managed by practice leaders for each area (e.g., pensions, benefits, compensation, etc.), who had significant autonomy over how they ran their businesses. I was the practice leader for our employee survey business, but in that role, I had to accomplish tasks through influence because I had no real authority. At a national meeting, Erica, the head of the eastern region, announced that she was implementing a new method for conducting employee surveys. It involved a shorter survey and a different report format. She talked about how great this new approach was and how it would be perfect for the kind of clients in her region.

As someone in the head office with responsibilities that cut across the firm, my default reaction to Erica's idea wasn't too positive. I was immediately thinking of the repercussions: "You can't do that! That will create chaos. We have standardized systems for a reason!" I had four reasons off the top of my head why it wouldn't work. I wanted to shoot the idea down before it emboldened other regional leaders to start their own processes. If I'm honest, I was cursing Erica under my breath for always wanting to have a different approach in her region. But I knew from experience that attacking Erica's idea or attacking Erica herself was only going to get her back up and encourage her to fight harder for what she wants. This was a perfect time to use the Impact technique.

Impact is an approach that draws the person's attention to a flaw in their plan that they are neglecting. Instead of criticizing a plan you don't agree with, the Impact strategy uses great questions to help the person come to their own conclusions about the risks inherent in their plan. For the person on the other side of the argument, it's much better to arrive at their own conclusions about the shortcomings of their approach than to have them pointed out by someone else.

To use the Impact technique, first ask an open-ended question to understand the motives underlying the person's plan, then reiterate what you hear to make the person feel you're listening. Next, ask a question that exposes an implication of the proposed solution the person hasn't thought of. Then explore other ways to address the person's original concerns.

Here's how it played out with Erica. "You're thinking of rolling out a new employee survey in the eastern region," I said. "What's leading you to that approach?" Erica had good answers: "Well, it's a few different things. First, our region has more competitors and we need to come in at a lower price point. Also, our clients are telling us that the reports are too long, and they want a more digestible format." Erica elaborated with examples of what the competitors were selling and made a pretty compelling case for the change.

Nothing she had said negated my biggest concern—her change to the format was creating inconsistency across the country. I raised the issue as gently as possible. "I can see why the change in format makes great sense in your region. How is it going to impact our national clients that work with us across regions?" Erica immediately grasped the problem. She wasn't defensive. She knew our national clients were important and that we'd have to figure a solution that worked for her region and for the whole country.

By following this approach, I heard and validated Erica's concerns about the current system being too bloated for her region. That kept the tone of the conversation constructive. It also helped her come to her own conclusions about the impact of her initial solution, so I didn't need to come off as the bad guy from head office. Conflict averted, on to problem-solving. We ended up creating a core set of questions that would be administered everywhere and then allowing regions to customize beyond that. That revised process stayed in place the whole time I was at the firm.

4. Hypotheticals

Another common conflict scenario erupts when you make a suggestion that is flatly rejected by a colleague. If the person blames their rejection on someone or something beyond their control, you're in the perfect position to use the Hypothetical strategy. What I mean by externally justified rejection is something like, "The technology team tried that back in 1997 and it didn't work," or "The salesforce will *never* go along with that!" The person is not willing to go along with your idea, but they aren't taking ownership of the resistance; they are deflecting the blame onto someone else.

Consider your most likely reactions to this scenario. You might dispute the basis of their resistance, "I think technology has changed a bit since 1997. Maybe it might be time to run this one up the flagpole again. Whaddayathink?" Alternatively, you might get frustrated with the person for blaming their resistance on someone else. "Are you kidding me? You're pinning this on the salesforce? If you don't like the idea, have the guts to say so." If you really don't like conflict, you might throw up your hands and give up. None of those is a great option.

The Hypothetical technique is based on the idea that exploring the upside of your proposal will make it desirable enough to overcome the resistance to the downside. The Hypothetical technique makes your end goal more desirable to increase your colleague's motivation to work through the barriers and objections.

To use the Hypothetical strategy, you start by validating the objection. (You're sensing a common theme now, aren't you?) I realize that when someone shoots down your idea, the last thing you want to do is validate them, but it's worth it. After you've validated the objection, park it and go around. Ask the person to imagine what it could look like if you magically managed to overcome the resistance. Once the person has started to see the benefit of the idea, return to solve for the objection.

An acquisition opportunity at a pharmaceutical company provided a great example of the value of the Hypothetical strategy. The corporate development team had identified a potential acquisition that could bring a new diabetes drug into the organization's portfolio. The numbers on the drug were fantastic and it was just the opportunity the company needed to boost flagging revenue. Unfortunately for the head of corporate development, Mark, the head of the product group, Dave, was not as enthusiastic. "We'll never get sales on board with adding a new therapeutic area [TA]."

Dave was not on board with the potential acquisition, but he was blaming his resistance on sales. He claimed the sales leadership would never go along with adding another area. Mark said, "Okay, sales will never go along with a new TA, gotcha. You're probably right." He paused, sighed, and then proceeded, "Okay, but just for a moment, play along with me. What if, somehow, I could get sales on board. What would be the value of having products in the diabetes TA?" It was an easy question for Dave to answer. Diabetes is a rapidly growing therapeutic area and one with a strong overlap with some of their existing drugs. Some of the key physicians and researchers in diabetes were already known to them through their current portfolio. Dave got more excited as he thought about these opportunities. That was a great point for Mark to enlist Dave's help. "I know Carole will take some convincing. How do you think we could pitch this to her sales team, so she sees the value of the opportunity?" In under thirty minutes, Mark convinced Dave that the acquisition was too good to pass up and enlisted him to help make the case to sales.

I wanted to use the pharmaceutical example to show you the power of the Hypothetical strategy for overcoming resistance in your organization, but my favorite Hypothetical story comes from my daughter, Kira. She was after my husband and me to get a new dog. Our old dog, Wilbur, a 135-pound Newfoundland, had died three years before. The kids who never walked him, never brushed him, and never fed him had decided that they *needed* another dog. I'd love to have a dog, but it doesn't fit in our lifestyle. Our girls are both competitive dancers and travel frequently to competitions. We also go on long adventures abroad each summer. A dog just doesn't fit in the equation.

One day, I was driving Kira to a dance class when she started in on me. "I know we can't get a dog because we travel so much." *True,* I think. *I'm glad she finally accepts this.* "But if you ever got another dog, what kind would you get?" I picture the dog of my dreams. "I'd definitely get another Newfoundland, but this time I'd get a female. Her name would be Widget. She'd be all black. And this time, we would definitely not let the dog up on the couch." I was practically turning the car toward the Humane Society when I realized what she was up to. She was using the Hypothetical strategy on me—to great effect, I might add. Well played, Kira, well played.

5. Common Criteria

This next technique is particularly powerful when you have a group of people all weighing in on a contentious decision. The Common Criteria technique delays the discussion of potential solutions until everyone has had a chance to weigh in on what they are looking for in a good solution. This technique is particularly useful when you know the discussion is going to be heated because different parties will be trying to solve for different things. Here's how I used it with an executive team.

The team was facing a really difficult situation with revenue down and costs rising. One business unit was particularly hit hard, staring at a $50 million hole in their plan. The GM of that unit was agonizing over the thought of reporting another quarter in the red. He was desperate to make the cuts to bring the costs in line with revenue. At the same time, the CEO was feeling torn. He didn't like the numbers, but he was even more frightened by the potential of a layoff to ruin the company's culture and kill their momentum. The GM was infuriated that the CEO wasn't giving him the autonomy to make the calls for his business. The CEO was frustrated that the GM was only thinking about his own unit.

They wanted to fight about which was the right plan, but I wouldn't let them start there. Instead, I gave everyone around the table a chance to share their motives and their concerns—but only their motives and concerns, not their proposals. The GM admitted he was mortified at the idea of going to the board with numbers in the red. The CEO expressed his anxiety that the company would lose its mojo. Then another leader added that no one had talked about what message a downsizing would send customers.

Before we even started talking about suggestions, everyone was feeling positive that the way we were having the discussion was going to lead to a good outcome. Everyone recognized their issues in the Common Criteria listed on the whiteboard. The list included the impact on revenue and on profitability, key talent and culture, customer and market perceptions. Fists unclenched, shoulders lowered as people felt more confident that their perspectives would count in the decision.

Once we had the criteria ranked, then we started to talk about potential solutions. Although at first, the situation had been set up as binary—do a layoff or don't do a layoff—there were actually a few options in between. For example, one solution was to divert people from the less profitable unit to a unit that needed more resources. Although this wouldn't reduce costs for the company overall, it would improve the financials in the ailing business unit and reallocate the cost in a spot where the revenue would justify it. We fleshed out four different solutions.

Once all the solutions and all the criteria for evaluating them were on the board, we systematically worked through each option, weighing the impact on each of the criteria. The conversation took a 90-degree turn. Looking at the numbers, they decided that they couldn't ignore the financial situation and they had to make the cuts. But the people advocating for the cuts in the first place were the first ones to talk about how they could implement the decision in a way to minimize the impact on morale, especially with the strong performers. Using the Common Criteria strategy often results in breaking the difficult decision into two parts: what is the best thing we can do, and how can we best implement the decision to take into account other issues?

The Common Criteria technique sets people at ease by reflecting what's important to them in the criteria that will be used to make a decision. Once they hear their concerns being validated, people are more willing to listen to the other factors at play. From that point on, it becomes an exercise in problem-solving rather than a fight.

6. Own the Misunderstanding

In each of the previous scenarios, you have a sense of what's causing the conflict. Sometimes, the person isn't making enough sense for you to even diagnose the issue. That's when the Misunderstanding approach comes in.

The Own the Misunderstanding approach works when you're on a different wavelength than your colleague. You can't make sense of why they're talking about an issue or how their points are relevant to the problem at hand. It's an especially good approach when you are out of sync with someone who has more power than you.

When someone throws in a total non sequitur, it's natural to get confused, frustrated, and eventually fed up. If the person is a peer or subordinate, you might even dismiss what they're saying and carry on with the discussion. Doing that will drive their resistance underground and likely incite passive-aggressiveness—creating more conflict debt. Instead of discounting the comments that don't make sense, take ownership of your lack of understanding. Don't assume that what the person is saying is useless or wrong.

Your team is in a monthly management meeting. You're talking about your Q3 gap when Mitch chimes in, suggesting that you back off two of your proposed sales promotions on your new products. You are totally confused. How is doing less marketing and promotion going to help us sell *more*? You ask Mitch to pause for a moment and get him to reframe his statement: "We're talking about a sales gap and I think you're suggesting that we do less promotion." Mitch is totally calm, because obviously this makes perfect sense to him. "Yes," he says, "I think we're bombarding our people with too many promotions and they don't know how to choose which one to talk about with our customers."

It's still not quite adding up for you. The sales people aren't pushing *all* of the promotions, but at least they have lots to choose from. You need more clarification. "Tell me how having too many promotions to choose from is contributing to our sales gap?" Mitch is very glad to be able to enlighten you. "Sometimes they choose the ones that are less lucrative for us but easiest for them to sell. I'd rather create focus and just have them driving hard on our two most profitable products." Now that you understand what he's driving toward, you can switch to another of the conflict strategies.

The Two Truths would be: "For you, this is about getting employees focused. For me, this is about driving more traffic into the stores. How can we accomplish both of these things?" The Impact approach would be: "How will pausing promotions on less established products affect their potential for growth?" Alternatively, you could go with the Root Cause technique by saying, "For you, this is about creating focus. I get it. How could we create focus without stalling the growth of the new products I'm launching?" Once you've cleared up the original misunderstanding, you can use several of the other techniques, depending on how you feel about what you learn.

Owning the misunderstanding works because it doesn't challenge the intelligence or the power of the other person. It leaves you in the subordinate position and attributes any lack of clarity to your misunderstanding rather than to the other person's unclear communication. That will make enough room for you to figure out what you're dealing with, so you can choose an appropriate strategy to continue the discussion.

NOW YOU HAVE six different techniques to get out of the spiral of unproductive conflict and start contributing to a solution. These techniques take some effort and practice, but once you become proficient at using them, you'll find yourself in far fewer unproductive conflicts. You will have cracked the conflict code. In the next section, I'll share two tools you can use to reduce the likelihood that you'll encounter these conflicts in the first place.

In Brief

- Once you've established a line of communication and created a strong connection, you are in a good position to contribute to a solution.

- Use the Two Truths strategy to validate the other person's priorities while adding your own. Once you have documented both truths, work toward a solution that solves for both.

- Use the Root Cause approach to demonstrate alignment on the problem when you want to offer alternate solutions.

- Rather than contradicting or criticizing a flawed solution, use the Impact technique to expose the risks of a plan and then redirect the person toward a feasible solution.

- Use the Hypothetical technique to overcome resistance by asking the person to imagine the benefits of a plan before solving for the obstacles.

- When you have multiple stakeholders with competing interests, use the Common Criteria approach to get everyone aligned on what a good solution would look like.

- When all else fails, Own the Misunderstanding and use enough clarifying questions to figure out which approach would help you resolve the issue.

PART III
CODIFYING CONFLICT

≋ INTRODUCTION ≋

IN PART II, I shared the Conflict Code, an approach that focuses first on setting the right tone before diving into the argument. Using the Conflict Code will transform many of your potential conflicts from adversarial arguments into calm and collaborative problem-solving sessions.

The Conflict Code—establishing a line of communication, creating a strong connection, and contributing to a solution—definitely works. It just takes a lot of effort. If you had to go through that process for every single conflict in your organization, you'd be exhausted. In this section, we'll focus on what you can do to systematize conflict so it's a part of the standard operating procedure of your team. We'll start by talking about how to neutralize conflicts by setting expectations for everyone on your team. Then we'll work through a process to normalize the tensions that if left unlabeled can turn into unhealthy conflicts. Finally, we'll talk about how you can create a healthy conflict habit that increases the frequency and decreases the impact of conflict until you hardly notice it at all.

NOTE: Chapters 7 and 8 focus on processes for your whole team. If you're a team leader, you can call a meeting and start working through them. If you aren't the leader of your team, you might want to share these processes with your manager and encourage them to give the tools a try. Whether you're a team leader or not, you will get lots of practical ideas you can put into place in Chapter 9.

■ READ THIS BEFORE YOU START PART III ■

I'M EXCITED that you've made it through the first two sections of the book! In Part III, we're going to dive into the processes and tools you can use to get your team out of conflict debt. This is where I'm going to share my secrets about how I help teams systematize conflict so that it takes less of a toll on their people.

I've given you full instructions in the chapters and the appendices, but if you'd like additional support in implementing these tools, please visit my website. There you'll find many free resources (more than 400 searchable articles on the blog) and even an eLearning version of a facilitated session you can use in your next team meeting.

I look forward to hearing your thoughts after you finish the book!

LIANE

P.S. Would you be a reviewer? A review on Amazon helps us get the message of productive conflict to more people. If you would take a couple of minutes to leave a review on Amazon, I would greatly appreciate it!

LianeDavey.com

7

CLARIFY EXPECTATIONS

THE LEADERSHIP TEAM of a Canadian government department is sitting in front of me at an off-site session. The team consists of five directors and their boss, the executive director. Frustrations are running high. The meeting is long overdue, but this is the first opportunity they've had to spend a day together. It doesn't take long for one of the directors, Maria, to tell me what's going on.

"This is such a pressure-filled job. Our portfolio, healthcare, is the highest profile in the whole government and the media is scrutinizing everything we say and do. Our team of analysts is junior, and as their leaders, we're the ones that always have to take up the slack. I'm exhausted."

"Tell me more," I encourage.

"Well, I'll give you an example from last week. I got a mistake-riddled brief at 6 p.m. that the cabinet minister needed to use at 7 the next morning. I had to stay up late fixing it. I'm doing the same thing multiple times a week and I'm burnt out!"

Maria's story starts with junior people doing poor quality work, which then leads to extra work for the leaders. I know better than to take this story at face value. People don't set out to do bad work, so there must be more of a backstory. Time for more questions. "Who sent you the draft of the minister's brief last week?"

"It came from the policy analyst who was assigned to the brief," she says.

"Oh, do the policy analysts report to you?"

"No, they report to the managers in the department, and the managers report to us."

I'm surprised. The frontline analysts are sending their work straight to the directors without it passing through their managers for quality review. This is problem #1.

I probe a little deeper. "What kinds of errors are you finding in the drafts you're receiving?"

"There are lots of issues. In the one I got last week, the analysis didn't include relevant precedent from other cases. It didn't capture the government's strategy or tune in the issues. Even basic stuff like the grammar and the formatting was terrible. It took me a couple of hours to fix a single brief. I was working on it until midnight."

"Let's back up. Tell me the story of this brief from the beginning."

Maria starts to recall last week's events. I'll give you the short version. The executive director, Cindy, had received a message from the cabinet minister's office on Thursday saying that the minister had agreed to give a speech the following Wednesday. Cindy forwarded the email to Maria and Maria sent it on to Robert, the manager of the policy analyst team, who passed it to Zack, the analyst who would write the brief. Zack received the request late in the day on Friday. At 6 p.m. Tuesday, when the draft was done, Robert had already left the office, so Zack sent it directly to Maria. That's when Maria felt she had to rewrite the brief, so it was suitable to send to the minister.

As she spoke, I could imagine poor Zack receiving the original email and scrolling past each successive version of "please deal with this." At the top, I picture Robert's message saying, "See below." Beneath it, Maria's saying, "Robert, can you have one of your people prepare this?" Cindy's saying nothing at all and including only her automatically generated signature, "Cheers, Cindy." At the very bottom, maybe there were a couple of paragraphs from the minister's office about the event. That's all Zack had to work from.

The entire situation was set up to create conflict. How many brewing conflicts can you spot? First, the leaders failed to provide context or define what good work would look like. Second, Zack accepted his assignment without clarifying what anyone wanted in the brief. Third, Robert, Zack's manager, didn't add any value in reviewing the document before it got to Maria. Fourth, Maria changed the document without engaging Robert or Zack in the editing process, thereby setting the whole situation up to happen again. The result was tremendous inefficiency and animosity in all directions.

Maria is disappointed in Zack because of the poor quality of work she received and miffed at Robert for letting the document get to her in such rough shape. Robert is frustrated with Zack for submitting poor quality work, while Zack is angry with Robert for only telling him what he expected after the fact. Robert is frustrated that Maria and Cindy were looking for something in the document that they had never asked for and that he couldn't possibly have known about. Each person is feeling hard done by and blaming everyone else for the situation.

Part of the problem is that without a standard way of clarifying expectations, you're left to initiate a conversation each and every time you launch into a project. That requires significant time and effort, which is a big ask in a busy work environment. You need a way to systematize these conversations so you don't have to repeat them every time.

The U Tool

Within a department, so many of the potential conflicts can be neutralized by clarifying roles and setting expectations before issues arise. When you carry expectations without communicating them, you set yourself and your team up for unpleasant conflict. If everyone is clear on their role and the value they are expected to add, they will be less likely to disappoint, or be disappointed by, others in the group. Another benefit is that clear expectations also allow people to act quickly and deliver high quality work.

I developed a tool and a process to help you clarify expectations on your team. It's called the U. I know, it's not the sexiest name, but don't let that fool you. The U is an amazingly powerful way of avoiding conflict while simultaneously improving the quality of work. I've included all the instructions for completing the tool with your team in Appendix A.

The U helps you document two things: 1) the different levels describe *what* unique value you expect to get from each layer in your department (including what you need from your superiors, what your team will add, and what you expect from the layers below you); and 2) the different sides (left and right) describe *when* value should be added—either up front as work is planned and delegated, or after the fact as work is reviewed and approved. Figure 7.1 shows a sample of a simplified U completed for the government department example above.

IF EVERYONE IS CLEAR ON ›**THEIR ROLE**‹ AND THE VALUE THEY ARE ·**EXPECTED**· TO ADD, THEY WILL BE LESS LIKELY TO **DISAPPOINT,** ≡ OR BE DISAPPOINTED BY, ≡ **OTHERS IN THE GROUP.**

The U is a great tool because it clarifies the expectations you have of others but perhaps have never made explicit. When you carry expectations without communicating them, you set yourself and your team up for unpleasant conflict. I encourage you to work through the U exercise in Appendix A to communicate what your team needs from one another to support effective execution.

FIGURE 7.1

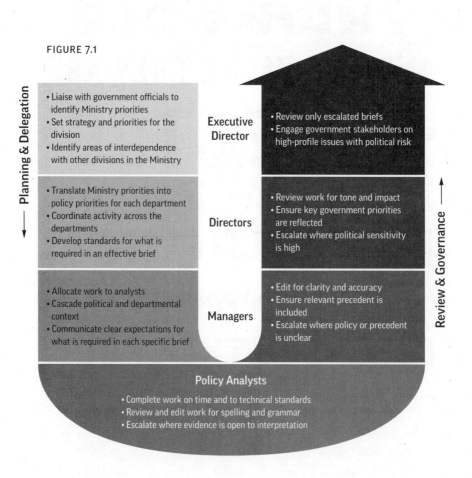

Common Issues

In the decade since I first developed the U tool, I have used it with dozens of teams. In each case, completing the U helps the team to understand the conflict that has been brewing and to make the changes that will stop conflict before it starts. Here are a few of the common issues you might be facing, and some suggestions on how you can use the U to neutralize the conflict.

You Have an Absentee Boss

One of the most prevalent problems I see is leaders spending too little time and energy as work is planned and delegated (on the left side of the U). This is particularly common in organizations where the list of priorities has ballooned, and the culture of busyness has taken over. You know you have this problem on your team if you can describe several kinds of value you *wish* your boss was giving you but isn't. That was the case in the example from the government department. Work was assigned with no context or direction and the result was considerable grief after the fact. I have come to realize how strong the connection is between the left and right sides of the U. Shortchanging the context and direction up front only increases the efforts in rework later. If you aren't getting what you need from your boss, the U makes a great conversation starter.

You can broach the topic as follows. "Lately, I've been noticing that our work is less efficient and effective than I'd like. We're revising a lot of work after the fact and it's causing friction on the team. To start to remedy this, we did an exercise to define expectations and get clearer on who needs to do what. One of the things that emerged was that I don't do enough to clarify your expectations and I think that's why we miss the mark sometimes. Let me give you a few examples of the information that would be valuable to get from you... How should I get this information from you from now on?"

Notice that you're not blaming your boss for not giving you what you need. Instead, you're taking ownership of not providing what your team needs. This is a version of the Own the Misunderstanding conflict strategy from Chapter 6.

If you want to be specific, you could provide an example to help your manager understand the impact of neglecting the planning side of the U. "When we submitted our plan for the new store opening last month, we hadn't included anything on the new fresh food format because we hadn't heard that the executive team had changed the strategy. We reworked the plan after the fact but that got us two weeks behind. How could I get more of that kind of information up front?" Focus on the business impact of shortchanging the planning. If you have a strong relationship with your boss, you could add some of the color about how it impacted morale to have to scrap several weeks of work. The main goal is to help your boss understand what she needs to provide for you to be successful.

One other possibility that might emerge if you share the U with your boss is that she tells you you're looking to her for too much; she's expecting you to make the call on some of the things you had originally thought of as her decisions. Just as you might be hoping for your direct reports to step up and take more accountability, your boss might be looking for the same from you. The U provides a great entrée to that conversation.

You Are Adding the Wrong Value

Perhaps the most common issue exposed by completing the U exercise is micromanagement, what I call "sliding down the U." If you have a problem with sliding down the U, you'll see it in two places. First, you'll see areas in your responsibilities that you're neglecting. You'll have activities in your left-side box that you're just not spending enough time on. Usually, these are issues that are longer term and more external in nature. These issues just aren't as pressing in the heat of the moment when you're trying to drive results, and they get less of your attention. Second, you'll notice that you struggled to differentiate what should be your responsibilities and what should be delegated to your direct reports (the activities in the third row down). That could mean that you're missing opportunities to empower them and impinging on decisions they could and should be making. After all, "admitting you have a problem is the first step."

Adding value at the wrong level can create considerable conflict in your team. First, when you neglect the strategic issues, you fail to provide the direction and context that your team needs from you. In this case, *you* become the absentee boss and set your team up to fail. The other issue is that as you dip down into issues and choices that should be made in the next level, you disempower the leaders whose job it is to be making those decisions. It's demoralizing when you do their job as it robs them of their opportunity to add value. I've even seen leaders more than two layers above encroaching on the work of the individual contributors. One of my clients admitted sheepishly that he had been "belly-down in the bottom of the U." He was simultaneously disempowering two layers of his team!

You need to tackle the problem of adding the wrong value in two stages. First, create a compelling case for why you need to spend more time on the responsibilities in your own remit. Talk with your team about the impact of neglecting these issues. Map out what types of discussions would be valuable and then create the forums where you can prioritize them above the pressing issues of the day. In my experience, you won't succeed if you try to cram these long-term, more strategic discussions into an existing meeting format; the urgent operational issues always seem to take precedence. Instead, map out an annual calendar of strategic issues and carve out at least a half-day each time to focus on nothing but the future direction.

The second issue you will need to confront is why you feel compelled to take over the work of your direct reports. This requires some soul searching. In some cases, the tendency to micromanage can be tied to a team that's still new or learning their roles. It's natural to get involved if you don't yet have confidence in your direct reports. But remember doing their job for them won't help them develop any faster. You can't learn to drive a car in the passenger seat. By getting too hands on, you're probably dooming yourself to do both their job and yours for the foreseeable future. Instead, create a plan to build their capability and gradually give them more and more autonomy.

Unfortunately, many leaders with a micromanagement problem don't have something as legitimate as a capability gap to blame for sliding down the U. Instead, they are stuck adding value at the level that they are comfortable with and are struggling to make the jump up to the next level of leadership. Often, I see this in leaders who prefer concrete, tangible tasks to the more abstract conversations, the ones who value expedience and action over deliberation and planning. If completing the U exercise helps you realize that you are adding value at the wrong level, ask yourself why and begin to make small changes that will redirect your attention. The longer you focus at the wrong level, the more conflict debt you will rack up.

Your Direct Reports Are Not Meeting Your Expectations

Another source of conflict often uncovered by completing the U exercise is that your direct reports are repeatedly not living up to your expectations. When this is the case, the conversations about the review and governance side of the U (the right side) become particularly animated. This is exactly what happened in the story at the start of the chapter. Maria felt let down by both Zack, the individual contributor, and Robert, his manager. Zack disappointed Maria by submitting a document that lacked the substance to be put in front of the minister. Robert let her down by neglecting his responsibility to provide the first-round review, which meant Maria had to revise both the substantive content and also the spelling and grammar. Somehow disappointment is even more toxic to a team dynamic than anger. Don't set up the people on your team to disappoint you.

If that is what's happening on your team, your energy and attention should be on setting the right expectations and then providing the support and resources that allow your team to meet them. First, use the U exercise with all levels in your department to communicate with one another about the value you're looking for at each level. Be open to hearing that your expectations aren't reasonable. You might learn that your expectations clash with competing priorities, scarce resources, insufficient capabilities, or other suboptimal realities. If you want to reduce the conflict on your team, you need to set expectations that account for all of these factors.

Even with the most reasonable expectations, your team might need more of your direction and guidance than you're providing. Ask for feedback about your management style. Is your team getting enough input and coaching to feel confident? If not, make a deliberate effort to check in more frequently to make sure people are heading in the right direction and at the right pace. Checking in gives you the opportunity to change tack if the current approach isn't working. Maybe the project needs more resources to achieve the goals. If you check in, you have the chance to change course before you wind up disappointed.

A cynical leader moves on after someone disappoints them, chalking it up as more proof that no one is trustworthy. If you want your team to consistently meet your expectations, you need to learn and adjust. Use the U to start a conversation about how you can build capability, improve communication, secure resources, revise timelines, and do the things that will make it easier for everyone to deliver instead of disappointing.

Deep Diving Bosses

Another common source of conflict on teams is a boss that overrides the layers below. What I mean by that is when a leader sees a result (e.g., a document, an angry customer call, a decision) that he doesn't like and goes straight to the source to fix it himself, skipping over one or more levels in the U. This is distressing for both the individual contributor who is confronted by an angry leader and for the manager who is left out of the loop. Fortunately, there are ways to reduce the friction created by deep dives.

First, recognize that deep dives are usually caused by leaders receiving unpleasant surprises. One way to reduce them is to have fewer surprises, with everyone involved understanding what types of issues warrant involving the boss. You can use the U exercise as an opportunity to talk about the importance of leaders setting thresholds during the planning phase. That means that as you are setting goals, each layer defines the range in which they are comfortable letting the next layer manage autonomously. For example, if you set a target such as $3 million per month in sales, they could say that they don't need to hear about it if one day is below the run rate, but if a three-day period falls more than 20% short of the run rate, then they'd like to be informed. These escalation criteria can be documented on the right side of the U.

Another simple technique to reduce deep dives is to create a template that direct reports can use when a result falls outside of the thresholds. This template should ask the first set of questions the boss would normally ask. That way, the boss knows that their direct reports are paying attention to the things they care about without even involving them. The template should work in conjunction with the measures of success and the thresholds. For example, if "below the threshold" means 20% below the $3 million run rate, the manager could fill out a template that includes prompts, such as, "For any sales results below threshold, comment on the traffic numbers and any other potential drivers (e.g., weather, holidays)." By having the right statements in the template, you can take comfort that the first level of analysis is happening without your involvement.

Once you've established these expectations about escalation, be deliberate about rewarding the right behavior. When one of your direct reports comes to you with a material risk to the company's financials, operations, or reputation, be quick to reward their disclosure. You might be upset about the issue, but if you get angry, you'll only discourage transparency in the future. At the same time, you need to discourage heroics. If you find out that a team member has been withholding information in hopes of fixing the issue before sharing it, you need to give unambiguous feedback that such behavior is unacceptable and that the result will be less autonomy in the future.

There will always be situations where you feel you need to be in the weeds. If a deep dive is required, follow these rules of engagement. First, unless the building is on fire, start by asking questions. Don't hip-check the responsible parties out of the way and fix the problem yourself. Second, assign one person to investigate the issue and bring the salient facts back to your team. Don't use meeting time to speculate about something you can't solve in the room. Third, notify any managers that you're talking to their people so that they can provide context to you and assistance to their teams. Fourth, zip it and listen to what people tell you. You're probably a little out of touch with how things work on the shop floor these days—so do more listening than talking at first. Fifth, once you've resolved the issue, close the loop with the frontline and with their managers. Don't let the same thing happen again. Doing the occasional deep dive is legitimate in our performance-oriented, high accountability work environments. Deep dive when you need to, in a way that minimizes unproductive conflict.

Your Team Is Feeling Invalidated by Feedback and Changes

One final source of conflict worth noting here is the gap in expectations about what will happen to a person's work after it's drafted. I'm surprised by how often people are upset by receiving feedback and suggestions from their superiors. I've witnessed people presenting to their leaders and becoming distraught when they receive input and requested changes. They were expecting a "good job" and a gold star. It's obvious that no one has bothered to align expectations for what should happen in review and governance.

The right side of the U documents the value that is added as work is reviewed and subjected to governance processes. Although high-performing organizations put significantly more emphasis on adding value during planning rather than waiting until something goes wrong, it's still important to clarify how draft work will be enhanced by successive layers of management, even when the layer below did their work exactly as intended. Unfortunately, some teams have set the expectations that leaders need to engage only if the work is of poor quality.

Fortunately, these misconceptions can be addressed with a conversation. Use the U to define what good work looks like and then to specify what value will be added even when the work is completed well. For example, I worked with a team leading an enterprise resource planning (ERP) software implementation. They built an excellent plan and submitted it to the chief information officer (CIO). He was really thrilled with the quality of their work. At the same time, because of his participation on the executive team, he was just learning about a record-high production schedule that would make the team's plan to train large classes full of people impossible to implement. He shared his concerns and the team worked together to build a plan that didn't require as many people to be off the floor at one time. If everyone knows what's expected of them from the outset, these types of revisions will no longer cause friction.

Other Issues to Explore

Here are some of the issues you can talk about now that you've mapped out your U.

1. What insight did you gain about how each of the levels in your department work together to optimize the output of the team?

2. Were there any areas where you found yourself slipping down the U and adding value in someone else's place? What impact does that have on the engagement of folks whose work is being supplanted? How can you spend more of your time at the appropriate level on the U?

3. Did you identify any levels where your expectations haven't been clear? What new appreciation did you get for that level? How can you communicate your expectations more clearly?

4. Do you tend to under-invest in the left-hand side of the U? Do you notice the repercussions in more rework on the right side?

5. Is there compression between your levels? Do you find yourselves adding value that should be added by the layer below you? If so, what's causing that? How could you get your level to stand down and the level below to step up?

6. Are you getting the value you need from the layer above you? If not, how could you broach that conversation to better set up your team for success?

Using the U with the Government Team

I want to return to the story of Cindy and her leadership team from the beginning of the chapter. Now that you understand the U, you can see how many of the conflicts on the team we could address with it. First, in Cindy's haste to initiate the work for the minister, she failed to provide any of the context about the government's strategy. As a member of the executive team, she had access to considerable information that would have helped Zack frame the key messages. After working through the U exercise, Cindy committed to taking at least a few minutes to provide this information when she is assigning work in the future.

Maria admitted that she and Robert had contributed to the problem by passing on Cindy's email without more clarification and also by revising the briefs without creating a feedback loop. Maria made several commitments that would make things more efficient and effective. First, she agreed that, from now on, she would use their weekly huddle to bring people up to speed on all the initiatives that were going on in the department, so they had that perspective. Second, she committed to prompt Cindy if she provided insufficient context. Third, she agreed to talk with Robert about her expectations of him as a manager and to be clear about what types of issues she expected him to address before the work got to her. Finally, she agreed she would share her edits and help the team incorporate them into future work.

As the discussion went on, multiple directors agreed that they were having the same problems with briefs not being up to par. They decided to ask one of their best analysts to prepare a lunch-and-learn session to help all the policy analysts improve their writing skills. That way, everyone would be clear on what was expected. They also set the expectation that the analysts should support and help one another to do great work.

These relatively minor changes created a major shift in the engagement of the team. Instead of frustration and disappointment, there was now a sense that everyone knew their role. Briefs were getting done on time and without the eleventh-hour interventions that had become standard. The whole department was happier and more productive.

The frenetic culture in many organizations causes leaders to shortchange up front planning to try to get things moving faster. The irony of this supposedly faster approach is that the time required to work and then rework is far greater than the time it would have taken to set up the work properly in the beginning. Not only does failing to clarify expectations slow things down, it also sets up an uncomfortable dynamic (i.e., one of judgment, disappointment, and negative feedback) after the fact, which has a terrible impact on both trust and morale. With a little time invested in completing the U, you can neutralize this unproductive conflict.

In Brief

- Failing to set clear expectations will lead to subpar work and inefficient rework, which creates frustration and conflict for all involved.

- The U tool helps you neutralize conflict by articulating what's expected of different levels in your department and when that value needs to be added.

- The U will help you get the value you need from your boss, while heading off unpleasant micromanagement and deep dives.

- Your team will have greater focus on your unique value and the activities that are most valuable for your business.

- Working through the U with your direct reports will allow you to raise the bar, while setting the expectation that you will challenge, critique, and improve your team's work, even when they do a great job.

8

NORMALIZE TENSION

I'**M WORKING WITH** the executive team of a large food processing plant. They have developed a rather unhealthy team dynamic, owing to a CEO with a penchant for public humiliation and the resulting self-protective behavior on the part of team members. Most of the individuals on the team are bright, collaborative people, but the unrelenting pressure to perform has taken its toll on their willingness to take one for the team.

I'm observing one of their weekly team meetings when a perfect example of their dysfunction comes up. The senior vice president (SVP) of sales is extremely excited that he has just received an order for a million racks of ribs for Independence Day weekend. One of the largest grocery chains in the country wants to run the promotion on the front page of their holiday flyer. This is fantastic news!

Or is it?

The SVP of operations is not looking nearly as excited. When I ask why, he points out the huge impact an order like this would have on his plants. "First, ribs are labor intensive, and we'd have to run one of our most expensive lines three shifts a day for weeks to produce this kind of volume. Second, it's not like pigs come as just a set of ribs, so what am I going to do with all the rest of the meat? I'm worried this is going to kill our efficiency numbers for the second quarter."

No wonder the operations leader is none too thrilled about the order. From his perspective, it's going to be a huge threat to hitting his objectives. It's easy to see why he's on his back foot. It's not only that the decision itself is causing friction, but the fact that it came to the team as a fait accompli feels offside. The SVP of ops is a strong team player and doesn't want to cause trouble, but this is definitely going to cause a headache for his entire division. He leans into and then away from the table several times as if deciding whether or not to say something. He's clearly conflicted about if he should fight this battle or just fall in line and suffer the consequences to his team.

This scenario is all too frequent: what's good for one member of a team is bad for another. Without the right forum, process, or language to move through the conflict constructively, many people shut down. Unfortunately, the issues and the animosity don't go away, they're just bottled up. The inability or unwillingness to constructively discuss the tensions on a cross-functional team can lead to passive-aggressive behavior and eventually to explosive anger and blaming. Ignoring the tensions doesn't work.

I am endlessly trying to convince teams that the secret to their productivity and engagement is to have *more* conflict, not less. Think back to before cross-functional teams were commonplace. Organizations used to do projects sequentially. Research and development would generate an idea, then pass it to manufacturing, then to marketing, and finally to sales. If sales or marketing had a concern with the product, it was a major endeavor (and expense) to back the process up to rectify it. Cross-functional teams bring all the parties together to create a forum for diverse perspectives to be shared, debated, and factored into an optimal approach. Conflict and tensions are not the *antithesis* of cross-functional teams, they're one of the main *benefits* of them. As the cool kids say, conflict is a "feature, not a bug." If cross-functional teams are designed for conflict, why isn't it happening?

When I try to understand the lack of team conflict, I immediately think about the Itty-Bitty Shitty Committee and their ongoing contribution to our lifelong conflict aversion. But they don't deserve all the blame. There are other voices telling us the exact same thing. The language and metaphors we use to talk about teams in the workplace are just as likely to dissuade you from disagreement. Our images of teams are all about getting along and going in the same direction, not about conflict. My personal favorite (and by that, I mean the one that drives me completely mad) is the office poster with a crew of rowers making serene and synchronous ripples in the calm blue water. It has the word "*teamwork*" emblazoned below.

What this image says to most of us is that we are "in the same boat," and to be good team players, we have to be "pulling in the same direction." We need a new metaphor.

The Tarp

It took me a long time to come up with one, but I finally found the story.

Several years ago, my husband, Craig, and I took our two daughters camping. It was a beautiful campground by a picturesque lake. All was well, at least until the weather forecast brought news of an impending storm. A *big* storm. Eyeing the flimsy rain fly covering our tent, I had visions of soaking sleeping bags and sobbing children. We drove to the nearest town to purchase a larger, more substantial tarp as added protection. I was willing to pay for a tarp to cover the entire campsite to avoid that horrible, soggy feeling. Since we were late to the party, the only available tarp was not much larger than our tent and would need to be strategically placed to provide any protection from the rain.

When we returned to the campsite, we unfurled the tarp and each of us took hold of a rope attached to a grommet at one of the corners. We proceeded to spread it out to cover as much tent as possible. Were we a team? Sure, we were. We had a common goal and we were interdependent. That's a team in my book (and this is my book). Were we pulling in the same direction? No. *No?* Wait, what? Exactly! You can be a team and not be pulling in the same direction. You can be a good team player and still create tension with your teammates.

Before I leave the tarp metaphor, our camping story can teach us a few more lessons. First, what happens if one team member pulls harder than the others? What if the strength of one member overwhelms that of his teammates? It turns out that he pulls the grommet right out of the corner of the tarp. And while he's at it, he sends the junior member of the team flying.

That's analogous to what happens on work teams, too. One person with a louder voice, greater power, or more knowledge throws the discussion off balance. Not only can people get hurt, but often the tarp doesn't end up over the tent... That is, the final solution isn't optimized for the business. Each team member must be careful to keep their participation in balance and not overwhelm the other team members.

There's another lesson from my story. What if one of the team members gets fed up, rolls her eyes, and walks away? What if she totally lets go of her rope even as everyone else is pulling with gusto? One side of the tarp goes flying and leaves a corner of the tent exposed. So that doesn't work either.

If one person doesn't pull their rope, maybe because they feel their minority perspective isn't valued, or because they are fed up with fighting, or because they are quiet and reticent to jump into the melee, we're back to the solution being suboptimized again. When one member of a cross-functional team stops putting tension on the discussion, an important part of the issue is left neglected and the team is exposed.

To get the best possible answer out of a team, you need to pull in different directions, always optimizing the tension on the system—never pulling so hard that you take the team off course, and never so gently that your angle isn't covered. That's what productive tensions should feel like.

I created a tool and a process you can use to map out the tensions that should be part of a healthy team dynamic. The Tarp tool helps you document two things: 1) the unique value you require from each role on a cross-functional team; and 2) the topics and stakeholders each role is advocating for that are in tension with those of other

≡ CONFLICT ≡
AND TENSIONS ARE NOT THE
▪ ANTITHESIS ▪
OF CROSS-FUNCTIONAL TEAMS,
THEY'RE ONE OF THE
MAIN BENEFITS
❭OF THEM.❬

roles on the team. The Tarp helps you normalize the tensions on your team so they don't lead to unproductive conflict. I've included all the instructions for completing the tool with your team in Appendix B. Figure 8.1 shows a sample of the Tarp completed for the food company with the rib order from the start of the chapter.

FIGURE 8.1

"We need lead time to prepare the workforce."

Human Resources
• Focus: employees
• Recruit and train staff
• Be prepared and responsive

Sales
• Focus: grocery chains
• Help grocers differentiate
• Be responsive and flexible

"We need to customize to win business."

Marketing
• Focus: consumers
• Provide tasty products
• Be new and interesting

Finance
• Focus: shareholders
• Optimize use of capital
• Be prudent and profitable

"We need to innovate to stay ahead."

"We need to optimize our resources."

Operations
• Focus: production
• Reduce waste and downtime
• Be efficient and safe

"We need to standardize to be efficient."

Learning from the Tarp

The Tarp is one of my favorite tools because it makes explicit something that you've probably felt many times . . . sometimes there's real tension among you! Thinking that everyone needs to be pulling in the same direction causes problems on teams. The image of rowers all rowing in the same direction gives the impression that it's wrong to dissent. When you spread out a tarp, you have a shared goal of covering as much ground as possible (e.g., the most revenue, the greatest customer satisfaction, etc.). To accomplish that goal, you pull in different directions and create tension with one another.

The tarp covers the most ground and stays on target when each person exerts the right amount of force. The situation breaks down if one or more people pull too hard on their corner, thus pulling the tarp off center or throwing the opposing person off balance; or one or more people pulls too gently or lets go altogether, thus allowing the tarp to get off center or leaving a corner exposed.

Each member of the team must understand which rope they're pulling (know the unique value of their role and obligation to the team). They need to pull their rope hard enough to exert some pressure on the team (speak up, disagree when necessary), while monitoring to ensure they're not pulling hard enough to cause harm (keep your comments focused on the issue and leave room for diverse perspectives). As a leader of a team, you need to actively manage these tensions.

There are many lessons to be learned through the Tarp exercise. I encourage you to explore them and to keep the discussion about healthy tensions going in all of your interactions.

Common Issues

Every team that uses the Tarp can get new insight into how to better manage their tensions. Some of these discussions are easy, while others unearth years of unspoken animosity associated with tensions that have been misunderstood and poorly communicated. Here are a few of the common issues you might uncover and how you can use the Tarp to normalize productive conflict among roles.

Someone Is Pulling Too Hard

One of the more obvious threats to a constructive cross-functional team dynamic is someone pulling too hard on their rope. You know you have this problem if one or two people dominate your discussions, either by taking up the majority of the airtime or by speaking loudly or aggressively. Overly assertive team members can sway a conversation toward their point of view and compromise the quality of the decision.

Completing the Tarp exercise with everyone on the team present will go a long way to exposing the offending party to the unique value of each diverse perspective. For many, this heightened appreciation will cause them to back off a little. If, after you've completed the Tarp, someone is still pulling too hard and skewing your decisions, it's important to get their contributions in check.

If the issue is that the person just talks too darn much, you can use formal approaches to rebalance everyone's contribution. Request material from each person that can be read before the meeting so the full range of issues are presented in advance. Use meeting agendas to limit the time for each function to speak. Shuffle the agenda to put the people or roles with less clout first. Use a formal decision-making process that requires you to capture each function's point of view before deliberating on the final decision. If the overly assertive person interjects out of turn, simply say, "We've had a first pass at the perspective from your position. I want to hear from each of the functions before we start a second round." Use whatever techniques are available to you to balance everyone's participation.

If the issue is less about time and more about tone, start with setting the ground rules for your discussions. I've had success with tacking this discussion on right after completing the Tarp. Ask everyone how you will need to engage with one another to make sure your discussions have the optimal tension. I go for the simple prompt, "To make the Tarp effective on our team, we need to do less ____ and more ____." This will create the opportunity for people to talk about the behaviors that pull the Tarp off center. While you're at it, develop your own safe language for calling out violations as they happen. It could be something as simple as, "You're pulling too hard."

If your early attempts to manage the unbalanced contribution as it happens don't work, it's time for some private feedback about the negative effects the person is creating by dominating the team. Try something like, "When we were talking about price changes this morning, you spent half the time talking about the revenue challenge if we don't get the price increase. I didn't get to hear enough from the customer-facing people about how a price change will affect them. As a result, I'm not comfortable proceeding with your plan. How could you make more space for the alternative perspectives in the future?"

As a manager, it's also worth doing some soul searching about how you might be contributing to this problem. If team members are pulling especially hard on their ropes, it's often because they believe their success is measured by how far they get their department, rather than on the quality of the decision for the whole team. They might be right. If goals and metrics focus solely on the person's contribution to their function, it's hard to blame them for pulling with all their might. A person rewarded only for revenue might be happy to sacrifice margins to drive sales. Start paying attention to what behavior you reward. Coach the person on the right balance between advocating on behalf of their function and having a team-wide lens. Find opportunities to recognize them when they make concessions that contribute to better solutions for the team. If you want behavior that puts team wins over individual wins, you need to stop sending the opposite message.

Some entire organizations are biased toward one side of the Tarp. I've encountered organizations where the sales function dominates every discussion, leaving gaps on operational issues and customer service. In other cases, control functions such as finance, risk, or compliance have taken over decision-making to such a degree that it's nearly impossible to drive growth. I mentioned earlier my deliciously witty client who referred to the head of risk and compliance as the "VP of business prevention." Biases that are baked into the culture are difficult to combat.

If your organization has this kind of a tilt, you will need to seed discussions about optimizing tensions at every opportunity. Use the Impact strategy from Chapter 6 to open a dialogue about the risk of over-indexing on one function. For example, in the case where sales is selling operations up the creek with promises they can't deliver, you might ask, "How will accelerating this sale into Q1 look to the customer if we can't fulfill the order for six weeks?" You won't change the culture in one conversation, but you will at least start to make the dominant team aware that there *are* other perspectives on the issue. Over time, you can educate them about the benefit of considering the other factors in their decisions.

Multi-incumbent Roles

If you manage a team with multiple people in the same type of role, it can be challenging to keep the perspectives balanced. I'm frequently called on to help with this kind of team because they are prone to unhealthy conflict. Examples include the leadership team of a retail bank, where the team is made up of six regional leaders plus one of each of the heads of the central functions such as product, strategy, HR, and finance. Another example would be the leadership team of an enabling function such as IT. You might have four business partners who work with the various business units and then the single heads of privacy and security, infrastructure, and architecture. When you have a team with multiple people in the same role, it tips the balance of discussions.

One of the problems with this structure stems from our basic assumptions that each person deserves an equal voice. If each person has an equal voice at a table with multi-incumbent roles, then the single-incumbent roles tend to get short shrift. Those four IT business partners go on and on about the problems with implementation while the central resources can't get a word in edgewise. This can lead to decisions that provide short-term benefit to the majority but ultimately put the team at risk by undervaluing the perspectives of the minority voices.

If you lead a team with multiple people in the same role, use the Tarp exercise to highlight this imbalance and discuss how to ensure your decision-making will give sufficient weight to all of the different perspectives. Actively manage the participation of the majority group by allowing only a subset of the group to speak before clarifying whether this perspective is representative of everyone in the majority group. "Okay, we've heard the same thing from two regional leaders. Do each of you agree?" Ask that only those majority members with alternative views add to the discussion before turning the floor over to those in different roles. This approach will help to ensure that your decision is based on all the facts and opinions, not just those from the dominant group.

Someone Dropped the Rope

It's not only those who over-contribute that hinder effective decision-making; it's also a problem when a member of the team under-contributes. You should watch for situations when one or more people stay silent or initially start debating but give up before the team has come to a mutually satisfying decision. When a member of your team stops advocating for their position, they deprive the team of the chance to consider all aspects of the issue.

As in the case of over-contribution, working through the Tarp exercise will shed light on the value and importance of every role. When the person who generally hangs back sees that keeping quiet does a disservice to their function, expertise, or constituency, they might be more inclined to weigh in.

If a given perspective is being underrepresented because the person doesn't speak up enough, you can use the same participation-balancing techniques you would use with someone who is over-contributing. Use pre-reads to share the thoughts of quiet team members, schedule time on the agenda for the person to share their perspective, or use a structured decision-making process that solicits input from each member of the team. While the person is still gaining comfort playing a more active role, you might need to prompt their participation with the occasional "Pat, we haven't heard from you yet." As the team leader, you can also make it easier for the person to interject by asking the more vociferous members of the team to pipe down.

If gentle nudges don't lead to sufficient change, you will need to provide private feedback. You can start with a tempered version, such as, "When we were talking about the proposed changes to restaurant layout, you didn't say anything in response to the reduced kitchen size. You're the employees' only representative at that table and we didn't hear how this change would affect them. How will you participate differently next time?"

Once the person takes ownership of their need to contribute more fully, you can offer to help. Ask what you could do to make it easier. You might learn that the way you chair the meetings or the way you participate exacerbates the imbalance in contributions. Be aware of your own biases and how you might inadvertently tip the balance toward perspectives you understand, appreciate, or that energize you. As the team leader, your job is to make sure all the relevant perspectives are factored in to create an optimal solution.

Sometimes there is an important perspective that is not represented by any of the people at the table, leaving your team vulnerable to poor decision-making. If you have a gap in the knowledge, skills, or perspectives of your team, as the team leader you need to find another way of filling it. If it's knowledge that you're lacking, you might find appropriate pre-read material to get everyone up to speed. If it's skills you're without, you might find a way to temporarily draft someone who can help. You can use contractors or consultants to fill a skill gap for the short term. If it's a perspective that you're missing, invite guests to represent key stakeholders in your meetings. In lieu of that, you can assign people to think like your customers, vendors, partners, or other stakeholders. Ultimately, if there is a mission-critical rope on your Tarp that no one is pulling, you need to change roles or team members.

Trade-Offs Are Not Managed

Once you work through the Tarp process, you'll realize how dynamic the tensions on a team can and should be. In the camping story, the tarp would need to be repositioned depending on which way the wind was blowing. The same is true of your Tarp. At various times, and for various reasons, one perspective might supersede another. That's part of the benefit of having a cross-functional team: you can negotiate these shifts with everyone at the table.

Where this process breaks down and causes considerable conflict is when things become too rigid. Annual goal-setting processes are one of the main culprits in constraining your ability to manage trade-offs across team members. That's because members of a cross-functional team are highly dependent on one another, but their goals are often set in isolation. It's ridiculous that everyone is depending on one another but has no visibility to what each person is on the hook for.

If this is the case on your team, it's probably contributing to conflict and mistrust. It's not hard to appreciate why. When a team member has clear line of sight to their own pressures and commitments but no appreciation of those of their teammates, it can feel like others are being willfully neglectful. To that team member, the rest of the team is unsympathetic and "just don't get it!" Similarly, when goals are shared but performance management is handled privately, it's common for people to feel that only they are being held accountable. Members of your team might passionately believe that you are cranking up the heat on them but not doing the same for everyone else. If you manage your team's performance behind closed doors, it's not surprising that they feel this way.

Using the Tarp tool helps manage conflict by clarifying expectations of what healthy tension on your team should look like. The Tarp works wonders when you have a team member who has been pulling too hard or conversely not hard enough. It helps you balance the dynamic when the people in multi-incumbent roles have been drowning out those in single roles. It even helps you understand and reverse the damage done when trade-offs among roles aren't managed. If you've faced unhealthy tensions on your team, the Tarp will undo some of the damage.

Our goal is not only to reverse damage that's already done but to prevent the damage from happening in the first place. To do that, you need to use the Tarp from the beginning.

Using the Tarp in Goal Setting

To make the Tarp process as effective as possible, you need to change how you set (and revise) performance goals. That doesn't mean you need to do all performance management in a group setting, but at the very least you should be setting objectives as a team. You can use this simple process to shift to team goal setting.

First, discuss your objectives with your leader to get the overall goals for the team as a starting point. Next, assemble your team and share those goals. Allot a couple of hours to discuss the goals and to consider the work effort required to accomplish them. After that meeting, have each team member work independently to develop two lists. The first list should include everything that person needs to accomplish for the team to be successful. The second list should include everything the person needs from their teammates to do their job effectively. Before the second meeting, distribute these lists as a primer.

Next, conduct a workshop where you address the following questions:

1. If we do everything on the lists, will we achieve our goals?
2. What additional objectives do we need to add?
3. Which proposed objectives will create work that is not a priority and need to be removed?
4. How should we prioritize the approved objectives?

As you answer these questions, you are creating a master list for the team and also allowing individual team members to revise their draft objectives accordingly. Following the workshop, each team member should submit revised objectives that can be shared, tweaked, and finalized.

Using the Tarp as a framework for setting goals is only the first half of the equation. It's an even more important conversation when things change and the original best laid plans are no longer valid. In most teams I work with, changes in the business environment or shifts in strategy or resource allocation have no bearing on people's objectives. Performance goals were cast in stone at the beginning of the year. When things change, everyone throws up their hands and thinks, *There goes my bonus!*

Imagine how much conflict this creates when those winds of change create a headwind for one team member and a tailwind for another. That was exactly the case in the ribs story at the start of the chapter. The windfall order of a million ribs meant the head of sales was in great shape to meet his targets, but the head of operations had no hope. To maintain a healthy dynamic on a cross-functional team, performance objectives should flex during the year.

I can share a story (modified to protect the innocent—and the guilty) that demonstrates this approach. The members of the executive team of a computer hardware company were setting their annual performance objectives. Terri, the head of PC division, was setting her goals. Her objectives were: 1) grow PC chip revenue by 7% while maintaining gross margins above 18%; 2) launch three new PC chips and secure design wins for them in 35% of tier one manufacturers' computers; and 3) increase customer satisfaction with all products to greater than 75%.

To be successful, Terri needed lots of help from her teammates. Her business was affected by the whole supply chain, including what price they paid for fabrication of the chips and how quickly engineering could get the product to the manufacturers. She was also dependent on marketing, who were going to launch her new products. There were also testing and quality assurance people she was counting on to get data she could use to make performance claims to the computer companies. She really needed everyone's priorities to be aligned.

And then real life happened...

A blockbuster product from a competitor meant the Chinese fabrication facilities were busy and could charge significantly more to manufacture the chips. The supply chain team was getting what capacity they could from their traditional suppliers, but it wasn't as much as they needed. Terri was loath to sacrifice quality, so she suggested sourcing from a different tier one supplier for a while. The head of supply chain wasn't thrilled with that idea because shifting suppliers would create more work and put them behind on their cost targets.

If that wasn't enough, launching the new chips was taking more effort from marketing than expected. Their competitors had beaten them to the punch with comparable products and it was costing more than expected to make minor modifications to optimize the product for each customer. That situation would have been manageable except that Terri's teammate, Stu, the head of the mobile division, had a hot new product and wanted marketing to focus energy there. Between the supply chain issues and the shift in marketing emphasis, Terri's goals were feeling like more and more of a stretch.

Terri told me how things would have gone in the past. Everyone would have become focused on their own targets and done what they needed to live up to their commitments—regardless of how that impacted the business overall. The supply chain leader was only incentivized on cost, so he would stick with the normal suppliers, even though that would threaten production. Terri and the marketing leader both signed up for three new chips so neither of them would have been keen to divert resources to a mobile product, even though that might be better for the company. Normally, everyone would have kept marching toward their performance targets and the result would have been a less-than-optimal year for the business overall.

Instead, I convinced the CEO that it didn't make sense to lock in performance objectives for a full year. Not only did he agree that they should adjust the targets in response to changes in the environment, but that changes to any one team member's objectives would trigger the team to re-open some or all of the others.

The team decided that it made sense for the company to hold back on one of the PC product launches and double down on the mobile opportunity instead. This decision was much easier to make when they made it as a team, with the flexibility to change individual objectives accordingly, than it would have been in the previous goal-setting process.

The same process can help your team. Rather than casting objectives in stone, maintain some agility by revisiting plans. Use your regular meetings to highlight risks to the plan in any part of the team. Anticipate issues as they emerge, while there is time to course correct. When one team member flags an issue (e.g., supply shortage, increasing cost of marketing) or an opportunity (e.g., new mobile product), the entire team should talk about implications. If it's warranted, revise the business plan.

Once you make the best decision possible for your organization, go back and revise individual objectives accordingly. If you choose to channel resources from one department to another, how will the personal objectives of the two leaders be adjusted to reflect greater or fewer resources? If you add work for one team based on opportunities that emerge, how will that affect their priorities? Does something need to be taken off the list? If you remove the conflict between doing what's best for your department and doing what's best for the team, you're much less likely to see selfish behavior and destructive conflict.

You might not be the head of PC division (or of anything else for that matter), but the same basic idea applies at every level. If your team members are dependent on one another for their success, you need to make decisions about what constitutes good performance together. If your company's performance management process doesn't work that way, color outside the lines. Nothing is preventing you from discussing and aligning objectives. If you can't officially revise objectives mid-year, at least make sure your boss and everyone else on the team is aligned with the decision to change focus. If you get penalized at the end of the year for doing what you all agreed was right for the team, your organization doesn't deserve you.

Cross-functional teams were built to bring together people with differing perspectives to allow them to efficiently and effectively work through the conflicts inherent in their work. What happens far too frequently is that your team is built for conflict, but the members of the team aren't. The conflicts that should be actively managed are instead driven underground. The tensions that naturally exist between roles are misinterpreted as personal conflict and the whole situation becomes uncomfortable and unproductive.

You can normalize the conflict on your team by using the Tarp exercise to map out the unique value of each role and the tensions that should exist among them. With heightened awareness and a shared language, your team will start to lean into these discussions, rather than avoiding them. The result will be better decisions and greater trust... all because you had more conflict, not less.

In Brief

- Tensions are a natural part of cross-functional teams, but many people misinterpret tension as contrary to teamwork. Failing to recognize the value of different and even opposing perspectives and priorities on a team can set up unproductive conflict.

- The Tarp tool helps you normalize productive conflict by articulating what's expected of different roles and how those roles will often be in tension with one another.

- Use the Tarp to coach team members who are under- or over-contributing.

- Address the imbalance caused by having a mix of multi-incumbent and single-incumbent roles on your team.

- Discuss the implications of making trade-offs between team members to reduce the friction caused by win/lose scenarios.

- Make use of the Tarp in goal setting to proactively manage the interdependencies on your team.

9

THE CONFLICT HABIT

I'**D BEEN WORKING** with a team on how to establish the foundation for productive conflict. In our first session together, the team was too far in the weeds to have a fruitful discussion. I learned that getting granular was completely normal for them. They had been meeting for eleven hours each week, including a four-hour Monday meeting where they reviewed giant stacks of paper with the previous week's results in six-point font. They dove into issues in such depth that even though the whole team was in the room, most conversations involved only two or three team members; everyone else just tuned out. Their typical discussions also lacked any perspective or insight.

I started by taking them through the U exercise from Chapter 7 to get them focused on the strategic issues. Getting them talking about issues that were more important and a whole lot more interesting helped keep everyone engaged.

Once they had a better sense of *what* they should be debating, we focused on *how* they should be debating. Initially, the discussions were dominated by a couple of strong-willed men who were accustomed to getting their own way. That needed to change. I worked with them to define their Tarp and map out what the healthy tensions were supposed to feel like. This idea didn't come naturally to some of them. The executive vice president (EVP) of customer experience kept telling people that he "owned" customer experience—implying that everyone else should bow to his will. We used the Tarp to help him understand that while he might be accountable for the overall customer experience, his peers who ran products and marketing (which controlled pricing) also had significant *pull*.

After considerable time and effort, the team was starting to have more constructive conversations. They'd come a long way, baby! They were talking about worthier topics and involving more people. They were more appreciative of the unique value each member brought to the table and getting better at the give and take of the Tarp approach. But the new behaviors were still fresh. Healthy conflict didn't come naturally—yet. The team was also still easily sucked into unproductive deep dives.

Knowing how hard they'd worked to establish this team dynamic, I was alarmed when I heard that the team was about to get a new leader, Jens. He was coming to North America for the first time after a long and successful career in Europe. I'd heard great things about him, including that he was very invested in creating a healthy team. But with a change in leader, especially one from another culture, I was concerned that the new ways of working might not hold. Jens hadn't even moved to the country yet and I was already on the phone with him, planning our first team off-site session. He said all the right things: how important his team is to him, how he hosts quarterly two-day sessions with a full day dedicated to team development, and how he can't wait to get started. It was music to my ears when he said that his goal was to create "juicy" conversations with lots of debate and dissent. Hooray! I'm all for juicy conversations.

The day of the first session with the new leader arrives. I drive ninety minutes out into the country to a beautiful, rustic inn. It's a picture-postcard kind of place with a babbling brook, a water wheel, and historic limestone buildings. It's already a big change from the downtown location where the team used to meet. Slowly, the members of the team arrive and take their seats around a horseshoe-shaped table. As the conversation begins, it is clear the team members are anxious. Their body language is much more closed than I'm accustomed to from this group. They look at the new boss and then look at me for direction (or just reassurance). They're sizing up their new leader and they aren't going to risk a misstep. If Jens is hoping for "juicy," what he's getting so far is dry toast. I'd warned Jens that the culture was not going to embrace conflict as readily as what he was used to.

Now he can see what I meant. The team members are quiet. They dutifully respond to questions, but they aren't volunteering any more than required. Jens can't stand the silence and is taking up way more airtime than I had hoped. He doesn't realize that by filling the silence, he's letting them off the hook. Now they're sitting back and waiting for him to provide the answers. I'm a little disappointed. It's clear to me that the conflict skills and processes I've helped the team build over the past year are not enough. We need to make productive conflict a habit.

The Conflict Habit

I was talking about productive conflict with my friend Dr. Marla Gottschalk, who's an insightful and influential organizational psychologist. Marla commented that facing workplace conflict requires a considerable amount of resilience. I agreed that the way we traditionally expect people to confront conflict (in endless difficult conversations) is a tremendous burden that requires great intestinal fortitude. My goal with every single team I work with, including Jens's team, is to teach a new way of thinking about and engaging in conflict that requires much less resilience. The goal is for productive conflict to become a habit: one you engage in routinely without requiring significant attention or effort.

That's the final step in embracing productive conflict. After shifting your mindset, building your skill set, and embedding conflict in your processes, your final step is to build a conflict habit.

Merriam-Webster defines a habit as "an acquired mode of behavior that has become nearly or completely involuntary."[15] That's exactly what you need to make productive conflict less taxing on you and your team. The secret is to increase the frequency and decrease the intensity of conflict until it becomes a habit that is so natural and normal that no one raises an eyebrow when a conflict emerges. When you develop a conflict habit, people stop taking things personally, their emotions no longer scuttle the conversation, and they don't bother getting defensive—they just work through the issue and move on. That's the ultimate goal: to make productive conflict a normal part of your workday.

There are endless ways that you can incorporate small changes in your behavior that will lead to healthy conflict habits. Here are five to get you started.

Habit #1: Clarify Expectations

I was sitting with the executive team of a telecommunications company. Their CEO had recently departed, and they were awaiting the imminent arrival of their new boss. I facilitated a session with them to help manage some of the tension that had emerged in the leadership vacuum.

We were discussing the executives' hopes and fears about what the new CEO would be like when one of the leaders, Ken, said, "I sure hope he recognizes how my business is different from the rest." I asked if he planned to share this hope with the new CEO. He said, "No," with a noticeable "Are you kidding?" tone. Ken said that it would be presumptive to tell his new boss what to do. I clarified, "I don't think you should tell him what to do. I think you should tell him what you'd like. There's a big difference." By holding this hope without communicating it, Ken was setting up his boss to disappoint him.

We do this to one another all the time. I call it the "Valentine's Day effect," because this is what so many of us do on Valentine's Day: we hold grand expectations of what would make us feel loved and appreciated, but we don't share these expectations with our partners;

instead, we wait for them to spontaneously deliver exactly what we were hoping for. Based on my informal polling, this is an ineffective strategy for receiving the Valentine's Day of one's dreams (more on this in the Bonus Chapter). Sadly, we do the exact same thing at work: we have a clear picture of what we want, and we wait for the other person to figure it out or, as happens more often, to disappoint us.

Holding expectations that you fail to communicate is a surefire way to create a conflict with your unsuspecting colleagues. If you want to avoid unnecessary conflict, make it a habit to communicate your expectations and solicit the expectations of others. From now on, start any new assignment (e.g., new job, new project, new task) with a conversation about what success looks like for everyone involved. Remember the principles of Chapter 5 and ask about the other person's expectations before sharing your own. Start by asking broad questions to leave lots of room for the answer to go in a different direction than you initially thought. For example, ask, "What would be a win for you?" or "What does success look like for you?" or "What needs to be included in a solution?" If you do this each and every time, your colleagues will start answering these questions without you having to ask. Clarifying expectations will become a habit.

Habit #2: Add Some Tension

When I give a speech about conflict, audience members often ask how they can introduce productive conflict to their conflict-avoidant team. I tell them that although productive conflict is healthy, it might not be appetizing right off the bat—a little like eating bran. If you serve up a big dry bran muffin of conflict, your team might take one bite and spit it out. Instead, sprinkle a few bran buds on their cornflakes. You can add low-intensity conflict to your team's diet with one or more of the following techniques.

TEST THE FACTS. As you're discussing issues or making decisions, your teammates will introduce information to back up their points of view. Instead of taking those facts at face value, do a little fact-checking.

THE GOAL IS FOR PRODUCTIVE • CONFLICT •

TO BECOME A HABIT: ONE YOU

> ENGAGE <

IN ROUTINELY WITHOUT REQUIRING

SIGNIFICANT

≡ ATTENTION OR EFFORT. ≡

"You're proposing that we roll out this program first to our high-end customers based on the idea that they are more digitally savvy than other segments. What are you basing that on?" This approach doesn't directly challenge your colleague's conclusions, but it does suggest that the team shouldn't automatically accept facts as given. If you do this all the time, it will feel less like you're questioning a single person and more like a standard operating procedure.

EXPLORE A DIFFERENT SIDE. If a conversation is narrowly focused on one aspect of a problem, you can introduce a little productive conflict by shedding light on a different angle. "We've done a good job at making this program simple. What could we do to make it sticky?" If you jump to the missing element, "That idea isn't very sticky," you'll find it chafes. Commenting on a legitimate strength of the argument and then adding a stretch won't feel as adversarial. Routinely exploring other sides of issues will acclimatize your teammates to having their ideas enhanced. They'll become less annoyed that you aren't accepting their suggestions in their original form.

REPRESENT A STAKEHOLDER. When your colleagues view an issue from a particular stakeholder's perspective, shift around to view it from a different point of view. "I agree completely that this program is going to be a winner for our customers. How do you think it's going to land with our operations team?" One caveat: you'll find this approach gets old quickly if you're always talking about the same group. Here goes Monika moaning about the marketers again. This technique is more effective if you switch up the stakeholder group that you advocate for. Keep a list of key stakeholders and mention one that isn't being considered in your team's deliberations. The Tarp exercise from Chapter 8 (and Appendix B) will help you map out the key stakeholders.

ADD A CONTINGENCY. Even if you agree with a plan that's forming, it's valuable to get people thinking about other ways the situation might play out. "I agree that's the way to go because I also think we're going to get our project to market first. How would the launch plan change if the competition beat us to market?" By encouraging your team to consider alternative scenarios, you'll expose assumptions, reduce groupthink, and help mitigate any risks inherent, even in a good plan.

DEFINE THE TERMS. One of the reasons that decisions fail to be implemented properly is that everyone has a different view of what they agreed to. You can reduce the likelihood of this problem occurring by asking people to define the words they're using. "We all agree that we need to increase the accountability in our leadership ranks by having more consequences. What do we mean by consequences?" Conflict-avoidant people tend to leave these kinds of terms undefined for fear of being seen as questioning authority. As we discussed in Chapter 7, failing to clarify expectations at the outset is only seeding a more uncomfortable clash later.

IMAGINE THE IMPLICATIONS. Help your team take their thinking one or two steps further by probing the impact of a proposed decision. "Okay, I think this plan makes sense. If we roll that out in the summer, where do we expect peak production? How will that play out?" This habit is great because it forces the team to think more proactively. Even if the plan has implications that aren't ideal, knowing what to expect will make it less likely that surprises trigger finger-pointing and blame.

SURFACE TENSIONS. As you listen to people discuss an idea, stay attuned to subtle differences in the language they use that might suggest they aren't fully aligned. Probe to see if you can improve their understanding. "I think I hear slightly different interpretations. Can we take another pass at what people think we're agreeing to?" If you have teammates who struggle to be direct about their concerns or disagreements, you will help considerably by catching these subtle differences in language that might reveal substantial misalignments.

HIGHLIGHT ASSUMPTIONS. One of the most dangerous things you can do in decision-making is make a bunch of assumptions without even realizing it. Helping your colleagues spot the suppositions on which your plan is built is very helpful. "This whole plan seems to depend on how this plays out in Michigan. What assumptions are we making about Detroit?" The point is not necessarily to challenge the assumption but rather to surface it, so that the team can decide whether it's legitimate or not.

MAKE ROOM FOR DISSENT. Sometimes you can't think of something specific to add to improve the quality of the discussion and the decision. In that case, make space for someone else's concerns. "What are we missing here? What holes could someone find in this approach? If someone in finance were to critique this plan, what would they say?" Your willingness to make room for dissent might be all that's required to encourage a quieter team member to speak up for the good of the team.

Using these relatively unobtrusive techniques regularly will start to build a productive conflict habit. Your goal is to increase the frequency and decrease the intensity of productive conflict on your team. Over time, you'll desensitize your teammates, allowing them to stay focused on the issue rather than getting distracted by taking disagreements personally. This way, you will work through issues as they arise rather than accruing conflict debt. Keeping a zero balance will put you in a much better position when more substantive disagreements arise because you'll be dealing only with the issue at hand, rather than all the baggage of unaired grievances.

To encourage you to use these techniques in every conversation, I've turned this list of ways to sprinkle conflict into a cheat sheet that you can tuck into your notepad. You can download a copy at LianeDavey.com.

Habit #3: Improve Your Feedback

Another aspect of building a conflict habit is getting into the routine of letting people know how their behavior is impacting you. If you don't provide feedback about the impact of your colleagues' actions, you start to hold a grudge. A grudge is—you guessed it—just another form of conflict debt. Getting good at giving feedback is essential if you want to avoid conflict debt. Withholding feedback not only incurs conflict debt, but it also starts to erode your credit rating. How can you expect your colleagues to trust you if you've been carrying a secret grudge without having the decency to tell them? It is time to make providing feedback a habit.

Unfortunately, if you're like me (and 95% of the leaders I meet), you probably struggle to give effective feedback. You've likely been delivering poor quality feedback and having to deal with the resulting backlash. The problem is that you load up your feedback with judgment—particularly judgment about what the other person thinks or feels, or who they are. As soon as you tell someone what they think or how they feel, get ready for a hostile reaction. Just picture someone telling you, "You are so negative about everything!" Does that make you curious, open, and interested in learning more? Not unless you're the Dalai Lama.

Rather than being filled with judgments, great feedback focuses on observations. The only legitimate thing you can say about someone is what you *see* because you have no reliable way of knowing what they're thinking or how they're feeling. In contrast, you know exactly what *you're* thinking and feeling, so that's fair game. So, to give great feedback, first describe objectively how the person behaved and then tell them subjectively how that behavior impacted what you're thinking and feeling.

Objective about them, subjective about you. Most people do the opposite. They assert subjective and judgmental statements about what the other person thinks or feels, or who they are and talk about the impact on them as if it were the objective truth. I made this mistake once. A member of my team, Sarah, was consistently looking at everything as though the glass were half empty. After one particularly unpleasant meeting, I made the mistake of telling her, "You think this plan is terrible and I can't have you on the project team anymore." (I told you I used to be bad at this!) My comment about Sarah was subjective (you think it's terrible) and the comment about me was framed as objective (I can't have you). Let me tell you, Sarah wasn't so thrilled. I was punishing her for *my* reaction—not good, Liane.

If you are inclined to tell someone what they are thinking, stop and reflect instead. Where is that judgment coming from? What makes you believe they are thinking that? I had to reflect on what made me think Sarah hated the plan. It wasn't hard to pinpoint what had set me off that day. I had shared the latest version of the plan that I got from my boss and Sarah raised three problems without mentioning a single positive comment. Once I thought about it, I realized I had missed a much better way to provide her with feedback. "When I shared the plan, you were the first to speak and you gave three reasons why it wouldn't work. This plan isn't an option for us, and when you started the conversation talking about what was wrong with it, it was really hard for me to get people focused on how to make it work. How could you contribute in a more balanced way?" As I came to know and understand Sarah better, I realized she was working hard to spot concerns and mitigate risks, but I blew my relationship with this smart and capable woman by pretending that I knew what she was thinking. It took a long time to earn back her trust.

If telling someone what they *think* is risky, telling them how they *feel* is even worse. Not only do you have no access to what they are feeling, you are now treading into emotional territory, which is even more sensitive. Examples of telling someone how they feel include, "You're getting frustrated," or "You're in a bad mood," or my personal favorite, "You're upset." First off, telling someone they are upset is most likely to lead to the response, "*I am not upset*," usually delivered with a red face and a strained voice. Follow that with your retort, "*Clearly* you *are* upset," and your fight has already begun. Instead, let the person know what you're witnessing that's making you feel like they're upset. "You've started three sentences without finishing. Let's back up so you can tell me how you're feeling about this." While you might think that observing someone's body language and tone gives you permission to tell them what they feel, it doesn't. Stick to describing what you see.

There is something even worse than telling someone what they think or feel. The most personal and offensive thing you can do when giving feedback is to tell someone who they *are*—to ascribe their behavior to some enduring part of their character. Prime examples are "You're lazy," or "You are such a bully," or "You're a nitpicker!" Accusing someone of not only *doing* something negative but *being* something negative is especially awful. If it's the first time you're seeing "lazy" behavior, it's not even appropriate to tie the person's actions to a personality trait. If you're recognizing a pattern of behavior, comment on that. "This is the fourth time this month that you have given me work that's missing one of the components we agreed on." For the person on the receiving end, getting feedback that challenges how they think of themselves is difficult enough when they're left to draw their own conclusions. Drawing those conclusions for them can damage trust in a way that will be difficult to repair.

To avoid building up animosity with your boss, your colleagues, or your direct reports, get in the habit of providing feedback. The discipline of spotting your own judgments and replacing them with better understanding is a highly effective means of avoiding conflict debt.

Habit #4: Use Humor and Code Words

Building a conflict habit doesn't have to be all somber and serious. As you establish the conflict norms on your team, build in some humor and use inside jokes and code words to draw attention to troublesome behavior in a gentler way. One team I worked with did this brilliantly. They had a leader who was prone to micromanagement. His propensity to get involved in the minutiae had the usual negative effects—it dragged him away from the strategic issues that needed his attention while simultaneously frustrating the people whose authority he was usurping. This leader, Lance, was super smart and really fun, but it still wasn't easy for his direct reports to tell him to butt out once he latched on to an issue.

I decided to introduce some humor to make it a little easier. Lance was particularly fond of the movie *Gladiator* and, on multiple occasions, showed a clip from the movie to his leaders. It was a scene where Russell Crowe's character, Maximus, orchestrates a battle from atop a ridge. He prepares the archers and the cavalry, laying out the plan of battle. But once things heat up, Maximus rides down off the ridge and onto the battlefield. Then he jumps off his horse and starts chopping off heads. Lance loved the motivational elements (his personal favorite was Maximus imploring his troops to "*hold the line!*"). Fortunately for me, this clip was a great metaphor for the issues with the CEO's leadership... Sometimes he would leave the high ground of leadership to get into hand-to-hand combat. After a really great discussion with his leadership team, Lance agreed that he needed to stay on the ridge.

Lance took the advice to heart and was very deliberate about when and how he involved himself. One day, a few months later, he slipped a little. The organization was planning a big corporate event. Members of the team three and four levels below the CEO were briefing the executives on their plans. A minor detail of the event planning came up and the CEO started intervening in the decisions, right down to "Should the gift basket for guests include a short-sleeved or long-sleeved T-shirt?" Lesser teams would have rolled their eyes and said nothing. To his credit, the chief of operations leaned over and whispered in Lance's ear, "Get back on the horse." He smiled and quickly changed his tune: "I'm sure you guys know more about this than me... whatever you think."

It was a small thing and it was a big deal. The CEO had effectively enlisted his team to help him sustain new behavior. Not only did employing a little humor help Lance recognize the issue, it actually helped them all laugh at something that had started out as rather infuriating. Since then I've heard all sorts of funny inside jokes used as non-threatening ways to convey important reminders about how people behave within their teams. Introduce some humor to make a dent in the issues without making a dent in each other.

Habit #5: Encourage Productive Conflict in Meetings

So much of the interaction you have with colleagues is in meetings, yet so many meetings have become horribly ineffective. Instead of creating a forum for productive conflict to be surfaced and resolved, meetings are often just hour-long displays of the power and politics on your team. The actual work of discussing options and coming to a solution is relegated to side conversations and the dreaded meeting-after-the-meeting. Changing how you manage your meetings is key for turning productive conflict into a healthy habit.

STATE THE PURPOSE OF THE MEETING. I'm always amazed at how much time is invested in meetings where no one really knows why the meeting is happening. We've become slaves to our calendars, mindlessly showing up at the allotted time in the cleverly named meeting room, filling the time with drivel until our phones chime and tell us to move to the next room. If you want to be productive, you need to break this fog. State the purpose of the meeting in the agenda and reiterate it at the start of the meeting. While you're at it, talk about what the meeting is *not* about. "This is our weekly operations meeting. We're focusing on issues that have a yellow- or red-light status. Anything with a green-light status needs to be held for our monthly review meetings." If you want them to eat their productive conflict vegetables, you have to take the dessert off the table.

SPECIFY THE PURPOSE OF EACH ITEM. Be clear about the kind of discussion each agenda item requires. If an agenda item is for information, say so and facilitate the discussion appropriately. Don't get into debates and don't go over the time limit—that wastes the time you need for productive conflict. If something is for decision, be clear on the decision criteria and specify whether everyone gets to vote or whether you're looking for recommendations and then one person will decide.

FILTER AND FOCUS. Ask people to filter their contributions and focus on points that add value. Don't waste time on violently agreeing with one another. "I'm looking for different perspectives and new ways of thinking. If you agree with what's been said, don't say the same thing over again." Remember conflict-avoidant teams will take any opportunity to have pleasant conversations instead of challenging ones. You will need to cut off endless agreement and compliment effective arguments.

REITERATE YOUR GROUND RULES. If your team has spent time developing ground rules (which I recommend that you do), then remind everyone about the most important ones at the start of the meeting. "Just a reminder that we've all committed to starting with a positive assumption and having conflict productively."

HEAD OFF PASSIVE-AGGRESSIVENESS. Be explicit at the start of your meeting that issues need to be addressed in the meeting, not after it. It's not a fail-safe approach, but if you call out difficult or contentious discussions at the start of a meeting and ask people to share their points of view candidly, it will increase the likelihood that you get the issues on the table rather than leaving them for hallway gossip later.

LEAVE 10% FOR WRAP-UP. I find it so demoralizing when a team has a great meeting and then ruins it by failing to create alignment at the end. Take the meeting seriously by setting a timer with an alarm to go off with 10% of your meeting time remaining. If your meeting is longer, you'll need more time to do a proper review. Set the rule that the person speaking wraps up and other contributions are held for the next meeting. "I know a couple of people were still in line to speak. Is this something we can continue over email or should we schedule time to discuss this issue again?" This approach will seem harsh at first, but the alternative is to waste the efforts invested in 90% of the meeting because you don't land them. Failing to ensure alignment also sets up nasty conflicts later.

REVIEW ITEMS AND RESTATE THE OUTCOMES. For each item, mention the purpose of the conversation, any decisions that were made, and the next steps, owner, and timelines for what needs to be done. Be prepared that stating these things explicitly might expose misalignment that requires clarification and sometimes even an additional meeting.

AGREE ON WHAT YOU WILL COMMUNICATE. Too often, it's left to the individual discretion of the people around the table to decide what they will and won't communicate. Leaving each team member to decide on what gets communicated can create misalignment and push conflict even deeper into your organization. Instead, draft the high-level themes that people should communicate and decide with whom they should be shared. Just as importantly, decide what isn't ready to be communicated and agree that those issues will be kept within the team until further notice.

EVALUATE YOURSELVES. Take one minute at the end of every meeting to gauge your performance. "How did we do? Was the time used wisely? Were we paying attention to the right things? Did we get to the outcomes we needed? Did we follow our own ground rules?" You don't need a seventy-two-item survey but getting a quick measure from participants and some thoughts on how to improve things for next time is a good habit to form.

SAY THANK YOU. If you're trying to encourage a conflict habit, take a moment at the end of the meeting to reinforce any positive changes. For example, "Thanks for being so open about the tough issues today, I appreciate your candor." Or, "It got a little heated there for a bit. I appreciate that everyone stayed engaged and talked through their perspectives."

Habits take time and effort to build, especially when they're designed to disrupt a pattern. Do the little things each day to clarify expectations, test for alignment, challenge with different perspectives, and uncover problems before they get out of hand. By adding a little productive conflict to each day, you'll wind up with fewer unpleasant, unproductive conflicts in the long run. If you're starting to establish a conflict habit, start small. Just because you have seen the light doesn't mean your colleagues, who might be more anxious about conflict, will appreciate your enlightenment.

In Brief

- The best way to keep conflict productive is to make small, frequent disagreements part of your daily habits. Begin to sprinkle a little conflict to help your teammates develop a taste for it.

- Invest time up front in clarifying expectations whenever you face a new task, a new project, or a new role.

- Make dissent more normal by adding tension to even the most routine conversations.

- Get more skilled at delivering feedback to help your colleagues understand the unintended impact of their behavior.

- Use appropriate humor and code words to keep difficult discussions light and to avoid triggering defensiveness.

- Set clear expectations for how meetings will support productive conflict, and use the start and the close of your meetings to reinforce those expectations.

A FINAL THOUGHT

ORGANIZATIONS DOLE OUT a steady stream of conflicts, from agonizing strategic trade-offs to petty interpersonal squabbles. You need to work through these issues to keep operations running smoothly. Giving in to conflict aversion and letting issues pile up will lead to conflict debt that stalls your organization, sabotages your team, and stresses you out. Instead, fight the good fight. Make the effort to establish effective lines of communication and build strong connections with your colleagues. Contribute in creative ways to come to solutions that, if not perfect for everyone, are at least the best choice given your constraints. You deserve to work on a team where productive conflict supports great decisions, strong relationships, and a positive working environment. Now you know fighting the good fight will give you the team you deserve.

≣ Bonus Chapter ≣

TRY THIS AT HOME

IN THE SPRING of 2004, I found myself sitting in a psychologist's office—the patient, not the therapist. My husband, Craig, sat facing me, and our psychologist sat perpendicular to the two of us. His office had just the right number of books to make him seem informed, without being pompous. They were strewn about, giving you the sense that they were actually for reference rather than decoration. His collection of furniture was cobbled together but each piece was functional, comfortable, and a little worn around the edges. The whole office subconsciously signaled that this was a place where you weren't expected to keep up appearances. What we were doing wasn't *tidy* work. To that end, the tissue box was strategically placed, visible but not central. By far, the most obvious accessory in the room was the giant clock—reminding me that I had only fifty minutes to make some headway on my marriage before retreating back to my solitude.

The specifics of what landed us in a psychologist's office eight years into our marriage are irrelevant. The fundamental issue was that we didn't know how to fight. As I told you, I come from a family where fighting just didn't happen. I had never seen conflict at home and assumed that great marriages (my parents' lasted sixty years) didn't include it. Craig was equally out of his element, coming from a family where the fights could get loud and personal. Neither of us had seen what healthy conflict looks like. We were both desperately afraid of hurting one another and as a result kept our issues bottled up. Our marriage was in conflict debt.

I still remember the mixture of apprehension and anticipation felt in the lead-up to each weekly session. Craig would pick me up from the subway and we'd drive in silence to the office. We'd park and hit the Starbucks, mostly to provide us with something to clutch during the unsettling work of counseling. We'd start each session speaking slowly and quietly, as if saying difficult things in hushed tones would make them less brutal. By the end of the fifty minutes, we'd be making real progress when the therapist would regretfully inform us that our time was up. The moment we stepped out of the office door, we'd recoil into silence, with seven days to collect the issues and grudges that would become next week's fodder. We interacted on the basic running of the family (we had one daughter at the time), keeping our conversations pretty basic like, "What do you want for dinner?" and "Where is Kira's backpack?" We kept quiet on anything more substantive than that.

Our silence was legendary. We could easily go a couple of days without speaking to each other. We fell into a pattern of ending these stalemates with the same small gesture each time. When one of us (we took turns in the role) was done being angry and ready to reconnect, we would simply ask the other, "Do you want a cup of tea?" Inviting me in for a cup of tea after I drove him home one night in graduate school was how Craig first showed he was interested in me, so offering a cup of tea connected us back to a happier, simpler time. Tea meant truce. It was better than nothing, but truces didn't solve anything. If we were going to restore our healthy marriage, we needed to break out of the cycle of anger, silence, and truce and start resolving some issues.

Over a number of months, we learned what we had never learned growing up. We learned to fight and to fight well. In retrospect, we were like kids who had never learned to crawl. The psychologist was teaching us basic things, but they were new to us. After one of our sessions, we kept talking in the car on the way home. We found the occasional issue we could broach on our own in between sessions. Eventually, our sessions were reserved for the most painful issues. I will never forget the day Dr. S sat back in his chair and watched us work through one of these difficult issues. He said, "You two are spectacular when you work together. You suffer in solitude." The same is true all these years later.

Today, we still tend to suffer in solitude. We are both conflict averse by default. But now we work hard to pay our conflict balance as we go—determined not to create conflict debt as we did before. Just as organizations churn out a steady stream of conflicts, so, too, does family life. Raising two daughters has supplied us with a great deal of practice!

It was Mother's Day, 2017. Craig was up and out the door very early to run the annual 10K road race near our house. We had agreed to that, and I was happy to laze in my pajamas until he got home. I'll admit that I had hoped our girls might spring from bed and shower me with affection, but three and a half hours after Craig left, he walked back in to find me at the computer and the girls still asleep. He tried to rouse them, but neither child seemed too concerned that it was Mother's Day. My hopes for a perfect Mother's Day were fading. I was getting more and more upset.

Now that it was obvious that I wasn't getting breakfast in bed, nor was I going to be treated to brunch at our local pastry shop, I threw a bagel in the toaster and used the time while it was toasting to work up some impressive self-pity. It didn't take long for me to realize that I was doing what so many people do—being angry with my family for failing to meet an expectation I never shared. I talked about this phenomenon in Chapter 9 as the Valentine's Day effect, but here I was proving that it works equally well on Mother's Day. I was mad at myself and decided to go for a walk to calm myself down.

The walk did me good. That, and a good cry. Of course, it was a bit awkward when I bumped into friends and had to explain my giant red puffy eyes, but all mothers understand that those moments happen. By the time I returned from my walk, I was feeling much better. The same could not be said for the family. Apparently, I hadn't communicated that I was walking to correct *my* mistake, not anyone else's. Everyone was in a tizzy. The kids were upset because no one had told them what was expected, because I was angry with them, and because their dad was agitated because I was agitated. Craig was frustrated with the kids for not getting moving and with me for being a drama queen. It was a bit of a disaster. We cobbled together a day out, but by then nerves were frayed and it was more about going through the motions than really enjoying our time together.

This year, Craig started early and encouraged me to talk with the kids about what I wanted my Mother's Day to look like. I told them that I didn't want gifts and that I didn't have anything specific in mind, but that I wanted to feel loved and appreciated. By the end of the day, that's exactly how I felt. The girls showed me they love me each in their own way, and Craig was there coordinating to make the whole thing happen. It's amazing how much better it is when you communicate openly and honestly!

Productive Conflict with Partners

The same principles apply to healthy conflict with your intimate partner as with your colleagues at work. Life presents a series of challenges that are bound to require tough decisions and conflicts. Do we go to the same restaurant week after week because it's comfortable and relaxing, or do we try something new to spice things up? Should we save money to have a down payment on a house sooner, or should we travel and enjoy our time before kids? I'm ready to retire and she wants to keep working... what should we do? Each of these questions, left unresolved, will be a fertile ground for resentment and animosity. Conflict debt is as crippling to a romantic relationship as it is to a professional one.

Clarify Expectations

The Mother's Day story illustrates the first principle of the conflict code at home—where possible, avoid it by setting expectations up front. The first step is to pay attention to what's important to you. That sounds funny, but we're often not conscious of what makes us happy, sad, or frustrated. If *you* don't even know what works for you, how do you expect your partner to know?! I have found journaling really helpful for reflecting on what situations trigger emotions and why. Once I've wrestled with the underlying issues, I can share them with Craig. It doesn't mean that everything always turns out exactly how I'd like, but when it doesn't, we both understand where my negative reactions are coming from and they're much less likely to create conflict.

Embrace Tension

Not all conflict in a relationship should be neutralized. Just as tension helps a business be more effective, it can help your relationship, too. Several healthy tensions come to mind. Take the couple where one person is highly spontaneous and the other is a planner. This tension probably ensures that spontaneous Steph remembers to pay the heating bill while fastidious Frank takes a break occasionally. A little tension between a spender and a saver is a good thing, too. As is a healthy balance between optimist and pessimist, risk-taker and risk-avoider, adventurer and homebody. The key is to talk about the differences, to appreciate the value of both perspectives, and to work to keep them in balance. Sometimes, that will mean appreciating your partner's needs and encouraging them to meet some of them without you.

Fight Clean

By clarifying expectations and embracing some tension in your relationship, you can neutralize most conflict and normalize much of what remains. Sometimes, it won't be enough. Some issues will be so upsetting, so intractable that you will find yourself in a real fight. The key then is to ensure that it's a good fight. You increase the likelihood that it will be a good fight by starting off the conversation positively. That means focusing on the value of your relationship, the importance of the issue, and your confidence that you can work through the issue if you stick together. You can try something like, "It's really important to me that we talk about where we're going to spend the holidays this year. I know I haven't done a good job of staying open and I'm committed to finding a solution that works for both of us this year."

It turns out that how you initiate conflicts is incredibly important to the health of your marriage. In a study by Sybil Carrère and John Gottman, researchers were able to predict the likelihood of divorce by listening to couples discuss a marital conflict.[16] Shockingly, it took only three minutes to differentiate the couples who would stay together and those who would break up (the study tracked the couples for six years). The difference was in how the conflict started. Couples who stayed married were much more likely to start conflict with positive emotions than those who eventually divorced. Although all couples became more negative as the argument went on, the couples who stayed married kept a mix of positive emotions. Other research from the Gottman laboratory demonstrated that healthy marital conflicts also focused on specific complaints ("You want to go to your parents' for the holidays again this year") rather than character-based criticism ("You're selfish and never think about what I want").[17]

Once you are into the thick of a conflict, take care to listen extremely carefully and reflect back what you're hearing. Investing effort in validating your partner's perspective will keep your argument below the boiling point. After your partner speaks, paraphrase what you're hearing and share what you're feeling. For example, "You're less excited about going to my family's because of how much travel it involves. You want a break at the holidays. I get that. It's really hard on me to miss out on our family traditions. How can we make it work for both of us?" You'll notice that this is the Two Truths technique from Chapter 6. Your partner wants to relax, and you want to partake in family traditions. From those two truths, you have so many potential solutions: alternate years, take extra vacation after the holidays to relax, visit your family at a less hectic time of year, or incorporate your family traditions into your own celebration. By validating your partner's needs, you'll revert to problem-solving mode rather than arguing.

Finally, in a long-term intimate relationship, it's easy to fall into the trap of thinking you know what your partner is thinking or feeling, and even easier to start assigning labels. That can be just as irritating and offensive to a partner as it is to a colleague. Being married to someone doesn't give you the right to tell them who they are. Plus, if you tell your partner over and over that he's boring, or boastful, or bad with money, you might create a self-fulfilling prophecy where he lives up to your negative expectation. After all, if he's already getting blamed for being "inattentive," he might as well keep watching the game! Instead, reinforce the behavior you appreciate. "I love when you sit and have dinner with me on Sunday nights." Focus on the positive. Remind your partner what you love about him, in case he needs a reminder.

Reframe Conflict

Don't measure the health of your relationship based on whether you have conflict or not. Instead, pay attention to the quality of the conflict. Do you communicate openly to make it easier for you to meet each other's needs? Do you frame difficult conversations with positive messages about how important you are to one another? Do you spend as much time trying to understand what matters to your partner as trying to convey what's important to you? Do you stick to describing the behaviors you want more of and less of rather than painting your partner's traits with a broad brush? If so, your conflict is strengthening your relationship, not hurting it.

Raising Conflict-Resilient Kids

One of the roles I'm most proud of is my volunteer work as a member of the board of the Psychology Foundation of Canada.

This amazing organization builds programs that help kids manage stress to keep them mentally healthy. You can learn more at PsychologyFoundation.org. We are supported by a variety of grants and donations, but one of our biggest resources is our annual fundraising breakfast. We fill a room with people eager to support us and to learn from an expert speaker about a timely topic in mental health. Last year, one day before the breakfast, our illustrious, hand-picked keynote speaker called the organizer, Cathy Backman, to tell her that he was too ill to travel. In a desperate pitch to have a speaker for the 400 paying guests, Cathy reached out to me and asked if I would speak. "Of course!" I responded, eager to help. After putting her mind at ease that she would indeed have a keynote speaker, I then asked, "What about?" It only took a moment for us to realize what I needed to talk about: the importance of teaching conflict skills to our kids. Conflict skills are critical for dealing with the inevitable stresses in life.

It turned out that I had a lot to say to parents, educators, and psychologists about our failures in preparing our kids for conflict later in life. Twenty years in the boardroom has made it clear to me the harmful effects of letting kids grow up without conflict skills. When I watch some of the parents of my children's friends, I fret that things are going to get worse. The bubble-wrapped generation is going to be in serious trouble as they reach the workplace. There are at least three areas where we need a significant change in how we parent or else our kids and our organizations are headed for a major meltdown.

Feedback

You have a responsibility to teach your kids to seek out and learn from feedback. Feedback is a critical source of self-awareness and one of the most valuable forms of development. Unfortunately, many kids are shielded from negative feedback by overprotective parents. Many of us are so obsessed with building our children's self-esteem that we throw ourselves in front of the feedback bullets that we think might destroy their fragile self-worth.

Here's the problem—we are the ones making it fragile! Self-esteem built on carefully curated rainbows-and-unicorns feedback is not real self-esteem. Real self-esteem is forged in genuine exploration of what you can and cannot achieve. Real self-esteem is strengthened by risk-taking, gumption, skinned knees, and bruised egos. The kind of self-esteem that comes from only positive feedback is false esteem. But finding truly constructive feedback for kids can be difficult. I know this firsthand. Both of my daughters are competitive dancers. There is no world where we distort feedback more than dancing. I remember my elder daughter, Kira, being awarded a gold medal for one of her performances. I was pleased as punch! Until I looked in the program and saw that gold was the fourth-highest level, below high-gold, emerald, and diamond. *What?!* And don't get me started on the five-foot-high trophy their studio brought home for fourth place!

If you are going to give your kids real feedback, you're often going to have to go it alone. Your daycare certainly won't help. I used to get a grocery bag filled with art each Friday night. (I use the term "art" loosely.) I remember one especially ridiculous inclusion: a piece of red construction paper with one purple paint line across it. My daughter Kira wasn't even old enough to sign her own name. The daycare teacher had done it for her. Was I supposed to display these masterpieces? At twenty pages a week, I would need a home the size of the Louvre. They were teaching my kids to be precious; they were leaving the dirty work of disposal to me.

We found a great solution. My mom bought the girls an art display hanger. It secured to the wall and had nine slots into which you could slide a letter-sized work. When a new bag of art came home, I simply asked whether anything in the bag warranted moving out something already in the hanger. When I shared this technique in a speech I was giving, one woman said that she disposes of the weekly art bag under the cover of darkness, hoping her kids won't notice the next morning. I took the opportunity to suggest that approach might be a titch passive-aggressive and that kids need to learn that not every brushstroke is worth saving for posterity. Sheesh... convincing people to give real feedback to their kids is harder than I thought.

Think of the consequences of shielding your kids from feedback throughout their adolescence. Are you going to travel with them to college or into the workplace? If not, that fragile, false self-esteem you've been guarding with your life will shatter the moment you aren't there to protect it. It has never actually become a part of your kid; it's only an illusion that you are projecting onto them: "You're the bestest you-est you that you can be!!!"

I'm not saying you should crush your child's spirit; I'm saying that you need to get real with them. When they ask you for feedback (children naturally seek it out), give them some. Here's my half of a conversation I had with my daughter, Mac, when she read me her speech and asked me if I liked it. "I'm so glad you shared that with me. What inspired you to write about that topic? I love your opening line—it really grabs me because I can picture it in my mind—what gave you that idea? I got a little confused when you moved from the first section to the second section—how could you make that transition a little smoother?"

She tells me she wasn't crushed by the interaction. (Actually, she said it was "fine.") Sure, she would have preferred in the moment if I had simply said, "Oh my goodness, that is the *best* speech I have ever heard!" But this way she had a chance to make it better before sharing it with her classmates. From the earliest ages, show your kids that you adore them and you're the person most invested in helping them learn and grow. Teach them to ask for, wrestle with, and ultimately learn from constructive feedback.

Practicing Conflict

The next thing that is going terribly, terribly wrong in our boardrooms is that we have no idea how to have conflict productively. We have the screamers, the eye-rollers, the sarcastics, the whisperers, but what's in short supply are the people who calmly and rationally put the different options on the table and work through them.

Again, we can see the seeds of this in our kids—and in our parenting style. On this one, I've been guilty. When my younger daughter was little, she told me about some unpleasant interactions with kids on the playground. My advice tended to be "just walk away." Now that can be perfectly good advice in some situations, but I realized I was teaching her to avoid conflict, rather than teaching her how to deal with it.

I righted my wrong the next time she reported a similar situation. "I had a fight with Sarah because she was cheating at hide and seek," she said.

"What did you say to Sarah when you saw that?" I asked.

"I told her that we agreed the field was off limits and she couldn't go there."

"What did she say?"

"She covered her ears and wouldn't listen."

"What do you find works to make things better with Sarah?"

She thought about it for a moment. "She needs a little time before she can talk about things. Sometimes I ask the teacher if she can help us problem-solve." Mac has always been pretty insightful about these sorts of things.

I encouraged her to nip the issue in the bud in the future. "What could you do next time you're setting out rules for a game that might make things work better?" I could see her really trying to work it out. She's motivated to make things better, so much so that she came to me to talk about how her other friend is totally different than Sarah and could I help her figure out how to deal with conflict with her.

I'm trying to teach her that conflict is normal, that she plays a role in it, and that she needs to be open and curious about how she can make it better. The goal is that she doesn't find conflict as aversive as most people do. Yelling "bullying!" at the first sight of a conflict is doing us a big disservice. Kids need to learn to differentiate between normal healthy conflict and harmful bullying and to deal with the run-of-the-mill playground issues on their own.

If you think I'm exaggerating about parents' allergy to conflict, I'll give you a truly kooky example. One of my friends was in her hometown for Christmas. She met up with her cousin, who was interviewing nannies for her eighteen-month- and nine-month-old children (yup, that math is truly frightening). She was looking for someone willing to adhere to her conflict-prevention approach (clearly a make-love-not-war type). Turns out that they have a gated-off area in their house and they rotate having one child at a time inside. The two kids aren't allowed to be together playing—they might get into a fight. If circumstance forces them to be together, an adult must always be sitting between them. Please tell me when and how these kids will learn how to have healthy conflict. The scariest part of the story is that the mother is a teacher! How many kids are learning a fear of conflict from her?

Learning to Be Uncomfortable

If there's a general problem with the people I meet on teams, it's that they just don't want to be uncomfortable. When they get close to something uncomfortable, they retreat at lightning speed. Again, I can see the origins in childhood.

We're teaching our children to avoid discomfort. Several years ago, my elder daughter had a young fourth grade teacher who took a pretty tough stance on the rangy kids in her class. If they didn't hand in their homework, they faced consequences such as losing their recess. Instead of letting the kids be accountable for failing to write down the homework, parents forced the teacher to build a website and update it daily with the homework so that they could keep track for their kids. Even that didn't satisfy them. That teacher lasted about six weeks before a group of parents forced her out of the school in tears, saying she "just doesn't fit in around here." Nope, we don't want our sweet little darlings to be uncomfortable!

The result was a revolving door of teachers for the remainder of the year—a travesty that many parents were enraged about (of course, they didn't take ownership for the fact it was a problem of their own making). I decided that it was a pretty close approximation to the real world and spent the time talking with Kira about how to make a first impression with a new teacher—a skill she had to use six times during that school year and one I'm sure will come in handy for the rest of her life.

At a more serious level, anxiety is reaching epidemic proportions in our children—it is replacing ADHD as the most common issue seen by child psychologists. Although the full story of how and why anxiety is proliferating is an issue for the scientific and medical community, it's clear that parents who respond to anxiety by protecting their children from the experiences they find stressful are only making things worse.

It is our job as parents to teach our children how to thrive. We have the opportunity to set the tone for a lifetime of experiences that will be challenging, uncomfortable, and even anxiety-provoking. If we make the mistake of trying to protect our children from these situations, we fail them in a very real and profound way.

As parents, we teach our kids how to manage money. They get allowances and learn to spend within their means. Unfortunately, we're not protecting them from conflict debt. We've given them our gold cards and they won't know how to function without them. Don't make that mistake. Teach your children to collaborate, to compromise, and to have conflict. There is no place they can end up in life where these skills won't be required. Every class we graduate without fundamental communication and conflict resolution skills will be at a great disadvantage.

Volunteer Teams

Now that I told you about the joys of being a part of the charity board I'm on, let me share a less-flattering observation about volunteer-based organizations: they can be cesspools of passive-aggressiveness. I have talked to so many people who tell me that their charitable organization has more conflict than their paid job. Instead of being a break from the pressures of the workplace, volunteer jobs can be more stressful than the normal workday. That's such a shame and definitely worth fixing.

High Tolerance

Many of my friends and clients put up with a considerable amount of dysfunctional behavior in their volunteer organizations. Do you? If so, what's behind your tolerance? The most common reason is that the cause you're working for is *so* important that it eclipses the petty infighting and poor team dynamics. You think, *Cancer is such a terrible disease. People with cancer suffer so profoundly. A little team dysfunction is a small price to pay for doing such important work.*

You might convince yourself to tolerate bad behavior in your volunteer team because people are giving their time away for free and it's not legitimate to expect that they behave a certain way. You think, *Karen is so sweet to give up her Saturdays every month to work at the nursing home. Who am I to complain if she breaks a few rules? The old expression holds when looking for volunteer workers: "beggars can't be choosers."*

Another huge problem in the volunteer sector is the lack of effective leadership. Maybe your organization lacks a leader who sets high standards. Many volunteer leaders don't know how to mobilize a group of volunteers to make an organization hum. Instead, everyone just pitches in and starts working. Unfortunately, these efforts are often poorly aligned. Important parts of the job are missed; elsewhere there's duplication of effort and stepping on toes. The lack of leadership hampers the ability of a volunteer organization to get things done.

Whether it's the importance of the cause, the generosity of the people, or the lack of leadership, there are many reasons why you might be putting up with crappy volunteer teams. Here's why you shouldn't. First, you're working on something really important. It matters. You need to get traction and make meaningful forward progress before [insert important cause: another child goes to school hungry, more people die of malaria, the school playground crumbles before your eyes]. You can't afford for the team to fail. You can't wait for the gossip circles and backroom string-pullers to finally come to consensus on what needs to be done. The more important the cause, the more critical it is that you get the issues on the table where they can be resolved.

You also can't afford terrible team dynamics because you're giving your time for free. This is your downtime, time you could be spending with your family, exercising, or binge-watching Netflix. You can't afford for your free time to be adding stress in your life. You need your volunteer time to charge your batteries and fill you up, not wear you down. You need the conflict to be healthy and productive.

Finally, you might not have the benefit of a strong leader to fix things on your volunteer team. You might need to contribute to a higher performing team yourself. Get it? All the excuses for why you *aren't* investing in a better experience on your volunteer team are exactly the reasons why you need to! Good news, you can use all the conflict skills and techniques in this book to change your volunteer team for the better.

Get Aligned

Start asking the right questions. Get everyone aligned around what you are there to do (and what is beyond your mandate). Ask, "What is the most important thing we're trying to accomplish?" "How can we add something unique to this very big and important issue?" "What kinds of requests do we need to say 'no' to so we can stay focused on our mission?" Get specific: are you a fundraising organization, an advocacy group, a caregiving service? Trying to be all things to all people isn't effective.

Volunteer organizations are very prone to scope creep—where anything that is worthwhile that could somehow be conceived of as part of the issue gets added to the list—and suddenly the efforts of the organization are totally diluted. Help create a conversation about focus. Redirect people to other organizations if their goals are too far from the core of the organization. Try saying something like, "This organization was founded to proactively address issues in children's mental health. While there are important issues for children who are mentally ill, not to mention critical issues of mental health in adults, I believe we can have the greatest impact if we stick to our focus on childhood prevention."

To Do or Not to Do

Even once you get aligned, scope creep will continue. You'll need to initiate frank conversations about what your team will take on and where you'll pass. Always connect your activities back to that mission. Get ruthless about prioritizing. That means you'll have to ask very clearly about what the team is *not* going to do. For example, "Our top priority is to provide meals to senior citizens who can't adequately feed themselves. Our second priority is to nourish them with a few minutes of company and conversation. Increasingly, we are being asked to provide routine help with other personal care issues. We want to help these people but I'm concerned that our best intentions might be taking up significant time, reducing the number of people we can provide meals to, and even increasing our liability. I propose that we refer these other requests to a partner agency." From experience, I can tell you that this will create conflict, but if you raise it the right way, productive conflict can be in the best interest of your organization and your community.

Feedback

Just because it's a volunteer organization, that's no reason to forego feedback. Your teammates are not being paid but that doesn't mean they get to do things that are counterproductive. Give feedback when someone is taking up too much time in meetings, when they are paying attention to the wrong things, or when they are treating you in a way that makes you feel uncomfortable.

Be calm, be kind, and be direct. "In today's committee meeting, you spent twenty minutes on the bake sale. That meant we didn't have time to talk about my dunk tank planning. Now I need to communicate with each committee member offline, which is far less efficient. How can you move through your items more quickly to allow room for other topics?"

Creating productive conflict in volunteer organizations is sticky. Your dedication to the cause tends to trump your concerns over wasted effort. You're grateful for people's time even if they are incompetent or counterproductive. You're doing the best you can in the absence of strong and effective leadership. But those are the same reasons why you personally need to take ownership and start contributing to a more vibrant and effective volunteer team. Align your goals, focus your efforts, and be transparent about what's working and not working. You deserve it!

And Everywhere Else

Your workplace, your romantic relationships, your parenting, and your volunteer work. If you could master productive conflict in those four domains, you'd have the most important bases covered. That said, you might also struggle with conflict debt in other situations, too. Families are rife with conflict debt. Maybe there's a sibling rivalry from your childhood that is still painful. Maybe Dad really did like him better? Or maybe your mother is angry with you because you don't visit enough. Sadly, some family conflict debt is passed on from one generation to other (at least financial debt dies with the holder). When you get less than your fair share in a will, or the family home gets left to someone else, your conflict with your mother is passed on to your siblings. That might sour your kids' relationships with their aunts, uncles, and cousins. It's so important to address family conflicts proactively.

It's not just organizations that require conflict—living requires conflict! At the dance studio, on the soccer field, with your contractor, at your place of worship . . . Conflict lurks everywhere. No matter where you are, the same rules apply. Neutralize conflict by being clear on expectations up front. When someone does or says something that upsets you, calmly and kindly give them feedback about how their behavior affected you. Make an effort to listen and reflect their perspective before trying to solve the problem. The more comfortable you become with conflict, the less it will wear you down. You'll pay your conflict balance as you go and never have to dig yourself out from under a mound of conflict debt.

ACKNOWLEDGMENTS

I AM GRATEFUL TO so many people who have shaped my ideas and, in the process, shaped me.

To my clients, who might recognize a few stories in this book, thank you for the pleasure and the privilege of working with you. It's because of you that I have the most interesting job in the world.

To the incredible group of people who helped me turn my clients' stories into a cogent and coherent book, thank you.

First, to the dynamite team at Page Two Books, you made this process so rewarding. Jesse Finkelstein, I'm so thrilled that the universe (and Martin Perlmutter's Facebook page) brought us together. Amanda Lewis, you are a gem of an editor; thank you for making my work better. Peter Cocking, you have my gratitude for bringing these concepts to life in design. Annemarie Tempelman-Kluit, thank you for helping me share these ideas with the world. And thank you to Gabrielle Narsted for making it all run smoothly.

Elizabeth Marshall, what a gift it was to meet you. You have such a deft touch. Your insights, wisdom, and encouragement were critical to making sure this was the book I wanted it to be. Every writer should be so fortunate to work with you.

To Amy and Michael Port at Heroic Public Speaking, where these ideas learned to crawl before they could walk, thank you for creating such a fabulous forum for passionate people to connect, learn, and grow. To the faculty, including the marvelous Mike Ganino, and the awesome AJ Harper, thank you for listening to the crazy lady who kept saying, "The world needs more conflict!" Thanks to my mentor, Antoine, for helping me realize it's okay to be a human mullet (business in the front and party in the back). Thanks to my aftercare crew, Josh, John, and Ahmed, and to Eliot, Jane, Corey, Joey, Melissa, Susan M., Ann, and all the other fabulous people from HPS grad school.

Thank you to Kate Davey for research assistance that got the ball rolling. Thank you to Cynthia Skilling for the U and Tarp graphics.

I am also incredibly grateful to the communities who give me the courage and confidence to believe I can change the world.

To the Speak & Spill community and our spiritual leader, Scott Stratten, I am so grateful. When I decided to strike out on my own, I didn't think I'd ever have the same type of community again. I was absolutely delighted to be proven wrong. While every S&S interaction provides that wonderful combination of learning and support, I want to give a special shout-out to the Montecito crew ("That will be nine kale Caesars and nine crispy chickens, please") especially gang leader, Mitch Joel. Thank you also to the SHIFT gang, rallied by Judson Laipply and Laura Gassner Otting.

Thank you to the team at my speakers' bureau, Speakers' Spotlight. Martin and Farah, you guys are the best in the business. To Bryce, Kelly, Dwight, and the whole Speakers' team, I look forward to many exciting opportunities.

Thank you to Ralph Shedletsky for your continued partnership and friendship and to kindred spirits Tammy, Jessica, and the Bobs (Sarah Skyvington and Mandi MacDonald).

Thank you to my mom for always being my biggest supporter (and the best proofreader there is). Thank you, Kira and Mac, for teaching me many of the lessons that I included in this book. Your insights about people continue to inspire and amaze me. Yes, I owe you. Yes, it can be a trip to NYC.

Finally, a simple thank you is not enough for my husband and business partner, Craig Easdon. You are the best teammate I could ever ask for. Thank you for your research, your perspective, your coaching, your support, and, most important, your companionship. I can't wait for all our adventures still to come.

≡ Appendix A ≡

HOW TO FILL OUT
THE U TEMPLATE

DOWNLOAD AND PRINT your copy of the U template under the "Books—Good Fight" tab at LianeDavey.com. You'll find both 3-level and 4-level versions. Choose the version that has as many layers as there are in your department. If you are a front-line manager (with individual contributors reporting to you), use the 3-level U. If you are two (or more) levels removed from the individual contributors (with managers reporting to you), use the 4-level U.

You'll see that the U is divided into layers horizontally to reflect the hierarchical levels in your department. Label the levels on the lines in the center of the U with the name of your team in the layer second from the top. Then put the name of the team above you (the team led by your boss) on the line at the top level. If you have the 4-level version, in the third level down, label the teams that your direct reports lead. The bottom layer is the "working level" where the team members are individual contributors.

Once you've got the levels of the U labeled, you're ready to begin.

You'll notice that the U has three sections corresponding to the different stages of work. On the left is where you describe the value of each layer in *planning and delegation*. At the bottom is where you

FIGURE A.1

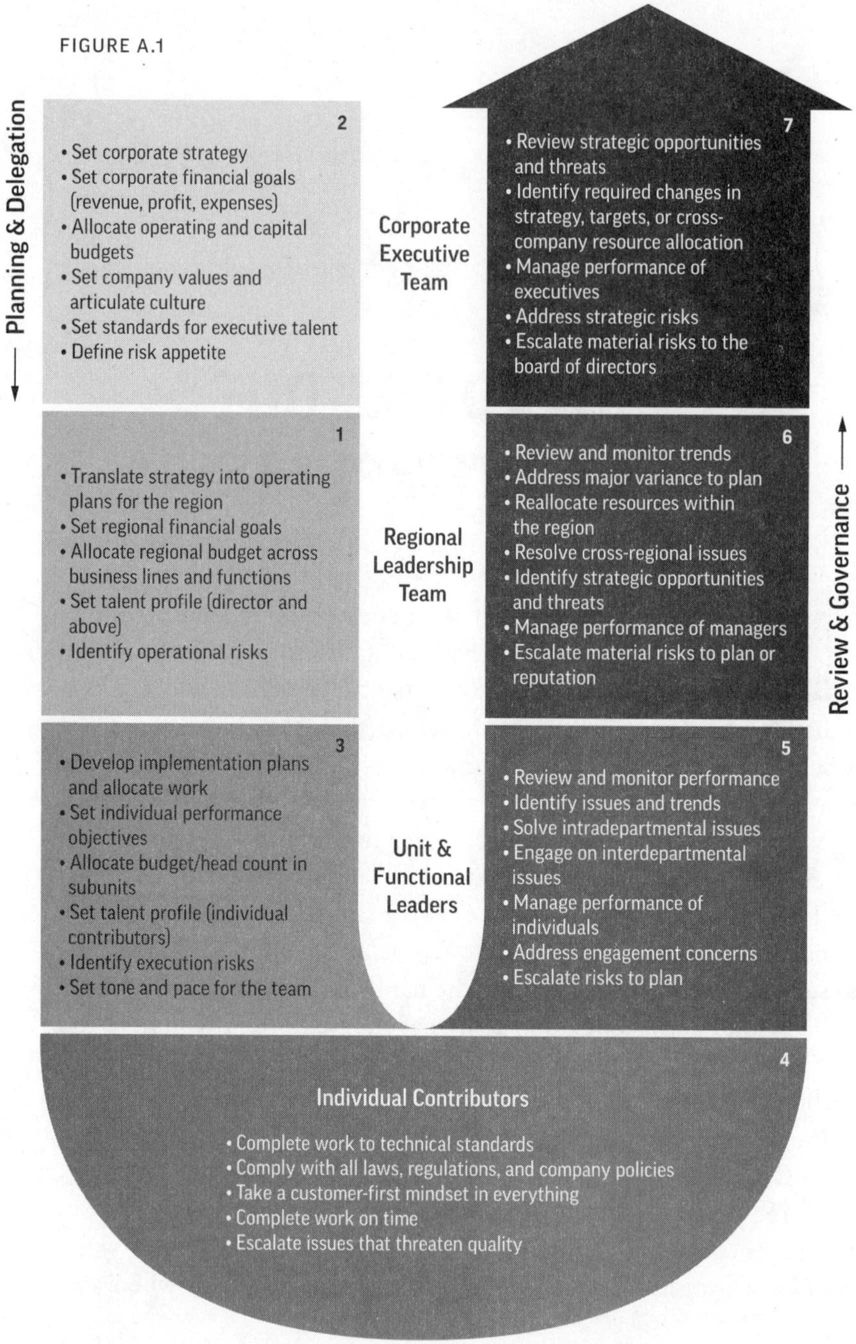

Planning & Delegation

2
- Set corporate strategy
- Set corporate financial goals (revenue, profit, expenses)
- Allocate operating and capital budgets
- Set company values and articulate culture
- Set standards for executive talent
- Define risk appetite

Corporate Executive Team

7
- Review strategic opportunities and threats
- Identify required changes in strategy, targets, or cross-company resource allocation
- Manage performance of executives
- Address strategic risks
- Escalate material risks to the board of directors

1
- Translate strategy into operating plans for the region
- Set regional financial goals
- Allocate regional budget across business lines and functions
- Set talent profile (director and above)
- Identify operational risks

Regional Leadership Team

6
- Review and monitor trends
- Address major variance to plan
- Reallocate resources within the region
- Resolve cross-regional issues
- Identify strategic opportunities and threats
- Manage performance of managers
- Escalate material risks to plan or reputation

Review & Governance

3
- Develop implementation plans and allocate work
- Set individual performance objectives
- Allocate budget/head count in subunits
- Set talent profile (individual contributors)
- Identify execution risks
- Set tone and pace for the team

Unit & Functional Leaders

5
- Review and monitor performance
- Identify issues and trends
- Solve intradepartmental issues
- Engage on interdepartmental issues
- Manage performance of individuals
- Address engagement concerns
- Escalate risks to plan

4
Individual Contributors
- Complete work to technical standards
- Comply with all laws, regulations, and company policies
- Take a customer-first mindset in everything
- Complete work on time
- Escalate issues that threaten quality

describe the value added in *drafting and editing*. On the right is where you describe the value added in *review and governance*.

BOX 1: Your Team's Value in Planning and Delegating

Start by filling in Box 1 (on the left-hand side, second level down). This box describes the value your team should be adding in the planning and delegation of work. The U is designed to help your department operate more effectively, so you want to list what value *should* be added, not necessarily what value currently *is* being added. Figure A.1 is a sample completed U for a regional leadership team.

With your team (i.e., you and your direct reports), answer the following questions:

1. What is the unique value our team adds at the start of the workflow?
2. What are others counting on us to decide before they can get started?
3. How do we provide the context required to ensure it's done right the first time?
4. How can we set everyone up to succeed?

You'll find many different themes within your answers. Think about strategy and planning. In the cascade between the CEO's team, where the overall corporate strategy is set, and the individual contributor who does the work, what is your team's role? If you're a regional manager in a retail chain, your team might take the overall product strategy and modify it to suit your location. If you are the director of tax, your team might translate the overall finance strategy into taxation approaches for different countries. As you discuss Box 1, you'll get a sense of the strategic decisions those in your department are counting on you to make.

In addition to strategy and planning, several other domains should be included in Box 1. Consider resource allocation—what resourcing decisions need to be made at your level? Some budget decisions will be made before they get to you—which are you expected to make? Think about goals, metrics, and KPIs and document the ones that you set. Include the decisions you make that affect talent and culture. Write your answers in Box 1 of your U.

When Box 1 is complete, you should have approximately ten ideas about how you and your team add value in the planning and delegation of work. The more specific you make your descriptions, the more useful they will be in clarifying expectations.

BOX 2: What You Need from Above

Next, fill in Box 2, which describes the unique value in planning and delegating of the level above you. Again, focus on what value you *should be* receiving from above, even if you aren't yet getting what you need. Include in Box 2 the decisions that are beyond your purview that set the context for your team.

Answer the following questions:

1. What decisions do we need from above to be able to build our plans?
2. What context do we need to make good decisions?
3. What resource allocation decisions do we need so we know what we're working with?
4. What factors does the layer above us use to define what success looks like?

Again, reflect on the different themes as you fill out Box 2. What strategic decisions need to be made by those more senior than you? What goals are set at layers above and then assigned to you? Document all the decisions you need your leaders to make so that you can do your job. Include anything that is beyond your authority including budget allocations, headcount, rewards strategy, risk appetite, and anything else you can think of.

A Note about Verbs and Nouns

No, don't worry, this isn't a grammar test. Just pay attention to the verbs and nouns that you're using in each of the boxes. You'll see that the themes run through all the boxes, but the specific verbs and nouns will change across the levels of the organization. Think of the strategy theme. Executives might set out the corporate vision and strategy. At the next level, leaders define the business unit or function strategy. Below that, the noun might shift from strategy to departmental plans. At the individual contributor level, strategy is set by creating objectives. You can see in the example of the completed U how a single theme cascades down the left-hand side and creates alignment throughout the company. For example, "strategy" appears at the top of the U, and then "operational risks" and "performance objectives" as the theme moves deeper into the organization.

Similarly, you might have a common noun all the way through the U, but the verb might change. Senior levels might "envision," while the succeeding levels might "build," "coordinate," and "monitor." Choosing these words carefully will help you convey exactly what you're expecting.

BOX 3: Delegated Authority (only for the 4-level model)

The third box describes the unique value you're counting on your direct reports' teams to deliver. Push your team to include as much in this box as possible. Too many leadership teams keep control of decisions that really should be delegated. Again, don't focus on what *is* happening, fill in this box with what *should be* happening!

Answer the following questions:

1. What decisions should we leave to our teams to decide?
2. What resource allocation decisions are we comfortable delegating?
3. What context do we expect them to provide to the people doing the work?
4. What do they need to do to set the individual contributors up for success?

Once you complete Boxes 1–3, you will have articulated the expectations of each level in planning and delegating work. You'll probably notice that there are several spots where your descriptions are aspirational, rather than accurate. Don't worry, that's the value of doing the exercise! Each time you identified an activity that isn't happening, or is happening but at the wrong level, you found an opportunity to make your department more effective. Keep going!

BOX 4: What Good Work Looks Like

Once you've finished the three boxes on the left of the U, switch gears. Instead of describing the value that needs to be added in planning and delegating work, now you're describing what good work should look like. You can use any criteria that matter in your organization or your team. The idea is to articulate expectations often left unspoken. That way, the individual contributors will know in advance what is expected of them.

Answer the following questions:

1. What is the basic standard of quality we expect in all work?
2. What do we expect to be included in work even before it receives its first review?
3. What are some of the things we catch during quality review that should be done properly from the start?

4. What types of questions or situations should cause individual contributors to escalate to their managers?

That fourth question is an important one. Although most of the points in Box 4 pertain to the value you expect employees to add, it's equally important to specify what types of issues you don't want them handling alone. Defining which issues should be escalated is a critical part of your risk management approach. For example, in a call center, you might outline what a great customer service call includes (e.g., a welcome, thanking them for their business, a review of their current bill) and also what types of issues you do not want the representative to handle (e.g., customers who threaten to take their business elsewhere). Document as much of what makes for high quality work as possible.

BOX 5: First Level Review

In the boxes up the right side, you will define what value each level *should be* adding in review and governance, as well as the types of issues you expect that level to manage autonomously. Also, by specifying when and where each level should escalate, you're also defining what value each level *should not* be adding.

The box second from the bottom on the right, Box 5, is the value you expect frontline managers to add as they review work for quality. Include all of the issues and concerns that you expect to be addressed in the first level review.

Answer the following questions:

1. What should first level managers be looking for in draft work?
2. Even if the draft is done well, what value should the manager add, over and above?
3. What types of issues or decisions do we expect them to address without involving us?
4. What types of issues do we expect first level managers to escalate?

One cause of friction is that individual contributors are sometimes hoping for a rubber stamp and a gold star from above. In many cases, even when work is done well, there is still value that can be added from people with greater context or experience. By describing this added value in the U, you can set the expectation from the outset and avoid the friction caused by getting unexpected feedback. More on that later.

BOX 6: Your Value in Review

The second box from the top on the right is the value you should be providing as work is reviewed and governed. As with all the boxes on the right side, it also specifies the areas that go beyond your purview and need to be escalated to the level(s) above you.

Answer the following questions:

1. What value should we be adding over and above what managers are adding?
2. What additional insight can we add based on our broader exposure in the organization?
3. What types of concerns should we be addressing at our level?
4. What types of issues do we need to escalate to the level(s) above us?

BOX 7: Decisions

The top right box describes the value that is added after you've already weighed in at your level. It should include all of the decisions that are beyond your authority and issues that are beyond your ability to resolve. Articulating the decisions that are beyond your control helps you to focus your time and energy on what you do control.

Answer the following questions:

1. What value can the levels above us provide that we aren't in a position to add?
2. What types of concerns or issues do we need to escalate to the level above us?
3. What decisions are beyond our control?

So, there you have it! You have completed the U. Now to start mining it for all the riches it contains (see Chapter 7 for specific examples).

≡ Appendix B ≡

HOW TO FILL OUT
THE TARP TEMPLATE

THE **TARP TOOL** allows you to map all the stakeholders in your cross-functional team and define the unique value they each bring. In doing so, you can define what the normal, healthy, constructive tensions are supposed to look and feel like when everyone is contributing optimally.

Go to LianeDavey.com and under the "Books—Good Fight" tab, download a copy of the Tarp template with the correct number of ropes. To figure out how many ropes you need, take the total number of team members and subtract one for the team leader. If everyone on the team has a unique role, then that will be the correct number for your team. For example, if there are eight members of the team, you'll need a seven-rope tarp.

Your team might have two or more members in very similar roles. For example, you might have two or more people who lead a territory, or two or more people who are business partners. If two people have very similar roles on the team, you can count them as one role (and one rope).

Once you've got the Tarp with the right number of ropes, you're ready to begin. Figure B.1 provides a sample of a completed Tarp for your reference.

FIGURE B.1

"Lock it down
so it's safe
and secure."

"We can't do
everything
all at once."

"Stabilize what
we have
before adding."

"Think about
the system
as a whole."

"Give me new, customized
easy-to-use systems."

Data & Security
• Governance of data usage
• Analytics and AI
• Safeguard all systems and data
• Focus: external threats

Project Management
• Project methodology
• Project oversight
• Project governance
• Focus: cross-functional teams

Systems & Applications
• Application road map
• Business applications
• System maintenance
• Focus: line of business

Architect
• Design the IT stack
• Integrate across departments
• Data, infrastructure
• Focus: internal IT

IT Business Partners
• Needs assessment
• System implementation
• Issue management
• Focus: line of business leader

NOTE: you don't have to lead a cross-functional team to benefit from the Tarp. If the tensions between your team and other teams are causing challenges, you can fill out the Tarp with your team representing only one of the ropes and the other teams you interact with in the other sections. For example, if you run a business unit team, you could have your team as one of the sections and then have HR, finance, compliance, and marketing as other sections. Thinking about where your team fits and empathizing with the varying perspectives and motives of other teams will help you have more productive conflict with your partners.

Start by labeling each segment of the Tarp with the name of a role on the team (or if you're filling it out for teams beyond your own, put the name of a team in each wedge). Then choose which lucky duck gets to go first and answer a couple of questions.

1. What is the unique value that this role brings to the team?
2. What are they "covering" on behalf of the team?

Write your answers in the section of the Tarp corresponding to that role.

Let's take the IT example in Figure B.1. The head of IT leads a team with two IT business partners and four central functions: architecture, systems and application, privacy and security, and the project management office. The team begins the Tarp exercise with the IT business partner role. They decide that the IT partners are there to ensure that infrastructure and systems are meeting the needs of the lines of business. They aren't the system design experts, but they are responsible for implementing the systems within the business. The IT partners also serve as a conduit between employees and the central IT functions, bringing in feedback about what is working and not working and where new systems or tools are required. We would write, "implementation, issue management, needs assessment" in the IT partner section of the Tarp.

Next, decide whether there are any particular stakeholder groups that the role is particularly attuned to. Document the most important stakeholder for each role in their section of the Tarp. Some stakeholders might be internal (employees, the board of directors, managers) whereas others are external (suppliers, customers, distributors). Many unproductive conflicts emerge because team members view decisions only through the lens of their key stakeholder and fail to see how things differ from another vantage point. Being explicit about your diverse stakeholders will help people appreciate the different perspectives and will encourage team members to optimize your team's decisions for everyone.

For the IT partner, the key stakeholder is the line leader for the business that they support. Because the IT partner is a member of the business unit management team, his attention is on issues from a business perspective. He's thinking about how technology can provide a strategic advantage and how it will affect the operations of the unit. We would add, "Focus: line of business leader" in the IT partner section of the Tarp.

Finally, think about how you'd label the rope for this role. The rope is a nice way of describing the tension that this role puts on the team. Sometimes I talk about it as though the person was a doll with a string... when you pull that string, they only have a few things that they say. Woody in the movie *Toy Story* either says, "Reach for the sky" or "There's a snake in my boot!" when you pull his string. I know no one on your team is as predictable as Woody, but I bet you can think of something that this role is always advocating for. What's their mantra?

Take the IT business partner. Around a table of IT leaders, the IT partners are often advocating for newer better systems with greater customization for the exact needs of their business. While the data architect would love to have one common infrastructure across all business units, the IT partner is advocating for systems that are unique to their unit's needs. In the case of the IT partner, you might label the rope, "More customized" or "More tools!"

When you finish one role, pick another role that is often in tension with the first one. Put that role on the opposite side of the tarp. Now go through exactly the same steps, fill in the unique value, and label the rope for the second role.

If we return to the IT example, as soon as we move to a central department role, the tensions become clear. While the IT partner is focused on maximizing the value of systems to the business, often advocating for shiny new toys, the central IT leaders are more focused on the cost, stability, and security. They would love to have less to manage. No wonder there is conflict on the IT leadership team.

Work your way around the Tarp, including the unique value, the key stakeholders, and the tension-causing label on the rope, until you've covered each role on the team.

Reflect on What You've Learned

1. What insight did you gain about how each role works to optimize the output of the team?

2. What did you realize about the unique contribution of each role (or team)?

3. What aha moments did you have about why you're always feeling in conflict with a particular person or role? What new appreciation did you get for the importance of that other role?

4. Is your Tarp skewed in a particular direction? What might be causing that? How could you rectify this imbalance for the benefit of the organization?

5. Is there a corner that you're not covering well? Is there an issue or stakeholder that you neglect in your discussions? How might you strengthen that corner of the Tarp?

6. What do you need to do as a team leader to make this situation work? How can you make sure that you've balanced the different tensions and come to the best answer for the organization?

≣ REFERENCES ≣

1   Wolff-Mann, E. (2016, February 9). "The Average American Is in Credit Card Debt, No Matter the Economy." *Time*. Retrieved from http://time.com/money/4213757/average-american-credit-card-debt/.

2   An alarming study of 8,000 managers from 250 companies reported in the *Harvard Business Review* revealed how rare it is for organizations to have clear priorities that they act upon. Only 11% said their strategic priorities had the resources they need for success, while 51% said they could secure resources to pursue opportunities outside the strategic objectives. The study also revealed that organizations aren't agile in the face of shifting priorities. Only 30% of managers reported that funds are shifted across units to support strategy, while even fewer (20%) reported that people were shifted across units. Sull, D., Homkes, R., and Sull, C. (2015, March). "Why Strategy Execution Unravels—and What to Do About It." *Harvard Business Review* 93, 3: 58–66.

3   Botelho, E.L., Rosenkoetter Powell, K., Kincaid, S., and Wang (2017, May–June). "What Sets Successful CEOs Apart." *Harvard Business Review*, 95, 3: 70–77.

4   Adkins, Amy. (2016, January 13). "Employee Engagement in the U.S. Stagnant in 2015." Retrieved from https://news.gallup.com/poll/188144/employee-engagement-stagnant-2015.aspx/.

5   Howatt, B. (2015, July 16). "The Long-Term Costs of Not Resolving Workplace Conflicts." *Globe and Mail*. Retrieved from https://www.theglobeandmail.com/report-on-business/careers/leadership-lab/the-long-term-costs-of-not-resolving-workplace-conflicts/article25527147/.

6   Padgett, S., and Notar, C.E. (2013). "Bystanders Are the Key to Stopping Bullying." *Universal Journal of Educational Research* 1, 2: 33–41.

7   Asch, S.E. (1951). "Effects of Group Pressure upon the Modification and Distortion of Judgment." In Guetzkow, H. (ed.), *Groups, Leadership and Men*. Pittsburgh, PA: Carnegie Press.

8   Gelfand, M.J., Keller, K., Leslie, L.M., and De Dreu, C. (2012). "Conflict Cultures in Organizations: How Leaders Shape Conflict Cultures and Their Organization-Level Consequences." *Journal of Applied Psychology* 97, 6: 1131–1147.

9   Williams Woolley, A., Chabris, C.F., Pentland, A., Hashmi, N., and Malone, T.W. (2010, October 29). "Evidence for a Collective Intelligence Factor in the Performance of Human Groups." *Science* 330, 6004: 686–688.

10 De Dreu, C.K.W., and West, M.A. (2001). "Minority Dissent and Team Innovation: The Importance of Participation in Decision Making." *Journal of Applied Psychology* 86, 6: 1191–1201.

11 Hansen, M.T. (2018). *Great at Work*. New York: Simon and Schuster, 185.

12 Pettigrew, T.F. (1979). "The Ultimate Attribution Error: Extending Allport's Cognitive Analysis of Prejudice." *Personality and Social Psychology Bulletin* 5, 4: 461–476.

13 Festinger, L. (1957). *A Theory of Cognitive Dissonance*. Palo Alto: Stanford University Press.

14 Gazzaniga, M.S. "Your Storytelling Brain." Big Think. Retrieved from http://bigthink.com/videos/your-storytelling-brain-2.

15 Merriam-Webster Online. "Habit [Def. 2]." (n.d.). Retrieved from http://www.merriam-webster.com/dictionary/habit.

16 Carrère, S., and Gottman, J.M. (1999). "Predicting Divorce among Newlyweds from the First Three Minutes of a Marital Conflict Discussion." *Family Process* 38, 3: 293–301.

17 Lisitsa, E. (2013, March 13). "Predicting Divorce from the First 3 Minutes of Conflict Discussion." The Gottman Relationship Blog. Retrieved from https://www.gottman.com/blog/the-research-predicting-divorce-among-newlyweds-from-the-first-three-minutes-of-a-marital-conflict-discussion/.

ABOUT THE AUTHOR

DR. LIANE DAVEY is a *New York Times*–bestselling author, a regular contributor to the *Harvard Business Review*, and the host of the ChangeYourTeam blog.

As the cofounder of 3COze Inc., she advises on business strategy and executive team effectiveness and has worked with leaders at companies such as Amazon, Walmart, Aviva, 3M, TD Bank, and Sony.

Liane has a PhD in organizational psychology and has served as an evaluator for the American Psychological Association's Healthy Workplace Awards.

Liane is married to her business partner, Craig, and they have two teenaged daughters.

LianeDavey.com

BRING **THE GOOD FIGHT**
TO YOUR TEAM AND ORGANIZATION

By now, you're probably ready to get out of conflict debt, but you need your colleagues to get on the bus. How can you do that as quickly as possible?!

◼ HERE ARE FOUR WAYS TO GET STARTED... ◼

COPIES FOR YOUR WHOLE TEAM: Buy copies of *The Good Fight* for your whole team and I'll send you a free PowerPoint presentation you can use to facilitate a discussion with your team. Easy peasy!

COPIES FOR YOUR WHOLE ORGANIZATION: Want to buy books for your entire organization? Contact me about bulk discounts and special offers, including custom editions which can include a foreword from your CEO. (I'll even change my author picture to me in your polyester uniform!)

SPEAKING FOR YOUR EVENT: Want me to give someone the stink eye so you don't have to? You find the event, and I'll bring the keynote. We'll show 'em the troubles that conflict aversion is causing and inspire them to pay off their conflict debt. Everyone wins!

TRAINING SESSIONS FOR EMPLOYEES AND LEADERS: Need a little more than inspiration to get your organization unstuck? Bring *The Good Fight* training into your organization either virtually or in person. Options range from a one-hour webinar on the Conflict Strategies for Nice People to a two-day workshop for leaders.

◼ LET'S START THE CONVERSATION ◼

Send me an email or reach out on social to discuss one or more options for your team and organization. I can't wait to hear from you.

info@3coze.com · 🐦 @lianedavey · in lianedavey